Kingston Ontario Book 3 in Colour Photos, Saving Our History One Photo at a Time

Photography
by Barbara Raué
2016

Series Name:
Cruising Ontario

Book 142: Kingston Book 3

Cover photo: 150 William Street, Page 56

Series Name: Cruising Ontario
Saving Our History One Photo at a Time in colour photos

Books Available in Alphabetical Order:
Aberfoyle, Acton, Alton, Ancaster, Arthur, Aylmer, Ayr, Bloomingdale, Brantford, Burlington, Caledon, Caledonia, Cambridge, Clifford, Conestogo, Delhi, Dorchester to Aylmer, Drayton, Drumbo, Dundas, Eden Mills, Elmira, Elora, Fergus, Guelph, Hagersville, Hamilton, Hanover, Harriston, Hespeler, Jarvis, Kitchener, Linwood, Listowel, London, Lucknow, Mono, Mount Forest, Neustadt, New Hamburg, Niagara-on-the-Lake, Oakville, Orangeville, Orillia, Owen Sound, Palmerston, Peterborough, Port Elgin, Preston, Rockwood, Seaforth, Sheffield, Shelburne, Simcoe, Southampton, St. Jacobs, St. Thomas, Stoney Creek, Stratford, Tillsonburg, Waterdown, Waterford, Waterloo, Wellesley, Wingham

Book 114-116: Waterloo
Book 117-119: Windsor
Book 120-121: Amherstburg
Book 122: Essex
Book 123-124: Kingsville
Book 125-127: Woodstock
Book 128: Thamesford
Book 129: St. Mary's
Book 133-136: Sarnia
Book 137: Petrolia
Book 138-139: Welland
Book 140-145: Kingston

Other Books by Barbara Raue

Coins of Gold

Arrows, Indians and Love

The Life and Times of Barbara
Volume 1: Inventions That Have Enhanced My Life
Volume 2: Entertainment That I Have Enjoyed
Volume 3: East Coast Trips
Volume 4: Olympics Have Always Intrigued Me
Volume 5: Wonders of the World
Volume 6: Caribbean Cruises We Have Enjoyed
Volume 7: Animals
Volume 8: Storms and Other Major Disasters in My Lifetime
Volume 9: Wars, Terrorist Attacks and Major Disasters

The Cromwell Family Book

Laura Secord Discovered

Daddy Where Are You?

Visit Barbara's website to view all of her books
http://barbararaue.ca

Table of Contents

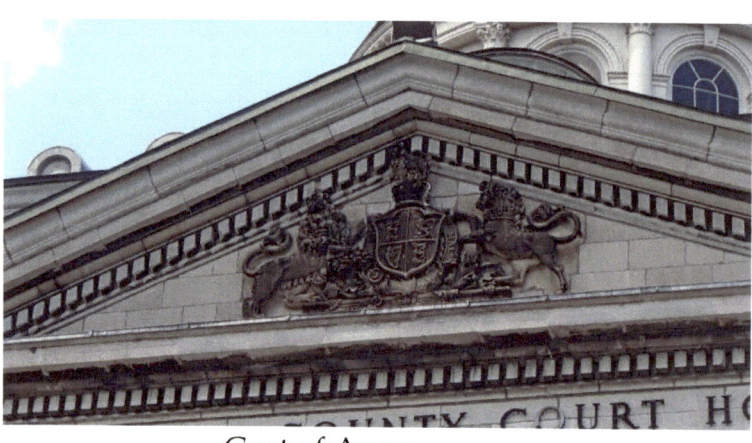

Coat of Arms

John Alexander Macdonald was born on January 10, 1815 in Glasgow, Scotland. His parents were Helen Shaw MacDonald, a Gaelic-speaking Highlander, and Hugh Macdonald, a struggling businessman. The family immigrated to Canada in 1820. MacDonald entered municipal politics in 1843 as Kingston alderman and was elected to the assembly of the United Province of Canada in 1844. He represented Kingston for 38 of the next 47 years. John and his wife Isabella Clark (died 1857) had two sons, John Alexander and Hugh John. In 1867, he married Susan Agnes Bernard who gave birth to a daughter, Mary. Throughout the years the Macdonalds lived in several residences in Kingston. He died in "Earnscliffe", his Ottawa home, in 1891.

In 1820 Kingston was the largest community in Upper Canada. With a population of 4,000, the town had a military base and an important port on the Lake Ontario-St. Lawrence River system. The Macdonalds were attracted here by the presence of Colonel Donald Macpherson, a military veteran who was married to John's aunt. Hosted by the Macphersons, the Macdonalds lived four years in Kingston before moving west to the Bay of Quinte area where Hugh Macdonald opened a store. John was schooled in Adolphustown until age 12 when he returned to Kingston to attend Midland District Grammar School. During this time he lived with the Macphersons, returning each summer to his own family at Glenora where his father had acquired a gristmill. In 1829, John enrolled in a new Kingston school for general and classical education run by John Cruikshank.

In 1830, 15-year-old John Macdonald was apprenticed to an established Kingston lawyer, George Mackenzie who entrusted him with opening a branch office in Napanee in 1832. Young Macdonald's responsibilities grew in 1833-35 when he was made manager of another law office in Hallowell (now known as Picton). Upon Mackenzie's death in 1835, Macdonald set up his own office and was formally called to the bar in 1836. In 1839, at the age of 24, he became solicitor for the Commercial Bank of the Midland District. Apart from practicing law, Macdonald invested in real estate and became director in several corporations with interest in banks, roads, and shipping. Macdonald survived the Depression of 1857 and the collapse of the Commercial Bank by relying on income from his legal practice and real estate investments.

First elected from Kingston to the Legislative Assembly of the Province of Canada in 1844, Macdonald was a leading figure in the public life of his country for forty-seven years.

During Macdonald's 47 years in politics (1844-1891), he was re-elected from Kingston thirteen times. In 1848 he resigned from the government to make way for the reform administration of Robert Baldwin and Louis-Hippolyte LaFontaine and was returned by acclamation in 1851. In 1856, John became leader of the Upper Canada section of the government of the United Province of Canada.

On July 1, 1867, the Proclamation of Canada's Confederation was read in Kingston's market square. The first federal parliament sat in Ottawa on November 7, 1867 with the recently knighted Sir John A. Macdonald serving as Prime Minister. During his political career, Macdonald presided over several Ministries: Justice (1867-1873), Interior (1878-1883), Indian Affairs (1878-1887), Railways and Canada (1889-1891). Under his leadership, the new Dominion was extended from sea to sea by incorporation of the territories of the Hudson's Bay Company, British Columbia, and Prince Edward Island, and linked together by the construction of the Intercolonial and Canadian Pacific Railways.

Macdonald's many connections in the Kingston community were influenced by his ethnicity, profession, and political aspirations. In 1835, he joined the emerging Celtic Society of Upper Canada, which later became Kingston's St. Andrew's Society, becoming its president in 1842. Macdonald joined such prominent local fraternal organizations as the Orange Order, the Free Masons, and the Oddfellows. He was a member of St. Andrew's Presbyterian Church and its active supporter in its initiative for a Presbyterian university at Kingston, Queen's University. Local development always figured in his politics and he championed Regiopolis Roman Catholic College, Kingston Hospital, the Wolfe Island, Kingston and Toronto Railway Company, and the scandal-ridden Kingston dry dock. As man about town, Macdonald used Grimason House (now known as the Royal Tavern) as his unofficial headquarters and meeting place.

Sir John A. Macdonald is remembered as a lively personality, a warm communicator, a consensus builder, a creative thinker, and a forceful leader. At the national level, he fought for unity through an integrated economy and the transcontinental railroad, becoming known as the "Father of Confederation". On the international stage, Macdonald strove to maintain the British connection and defend the frontiers of Canada against United States expansionism. Many things have changed since his time in office, but many of contemporary Canada's defining features, institutions and challenges have their roots in Macdonald's tenure as Prime Minister.

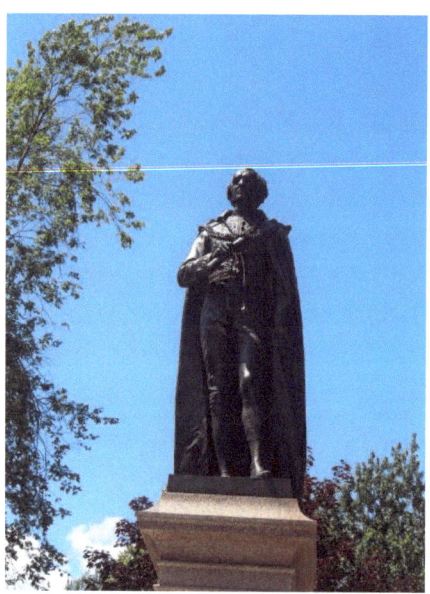

Statue located at the corner of King and West Streets with two cannons flanking it

The Cataraqui River forms the lower portion of the Rideau Canal and drains into Lake Ontario at Kingston. The name is taken from the original name for Kingston.

Cataraqui – rural village to the west – now part of Kingston

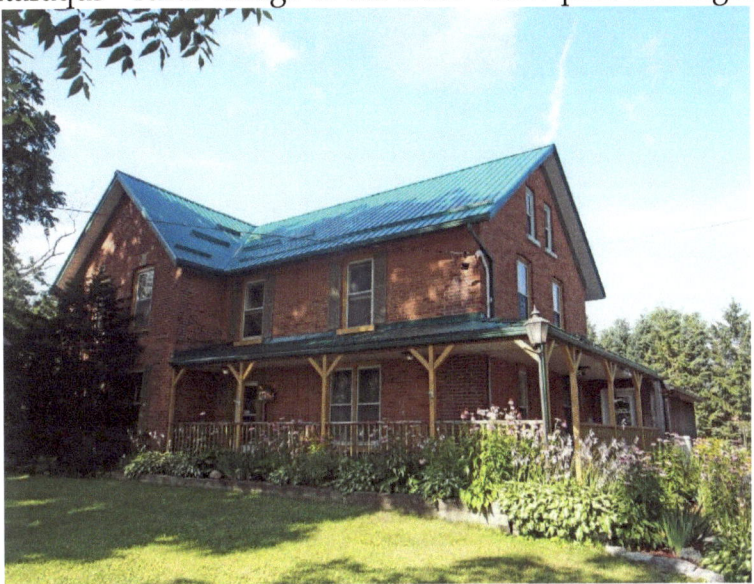

991 Sydenham Road – The Glass House

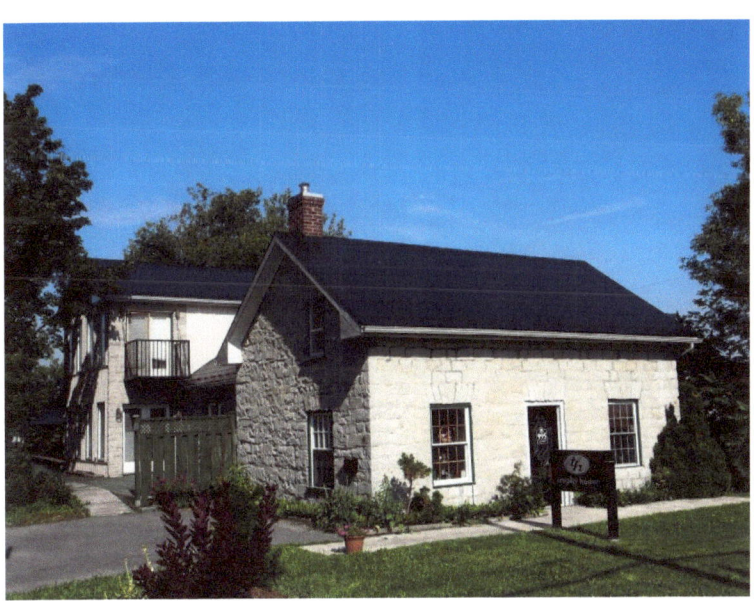

995 Sydenham Road - limestone

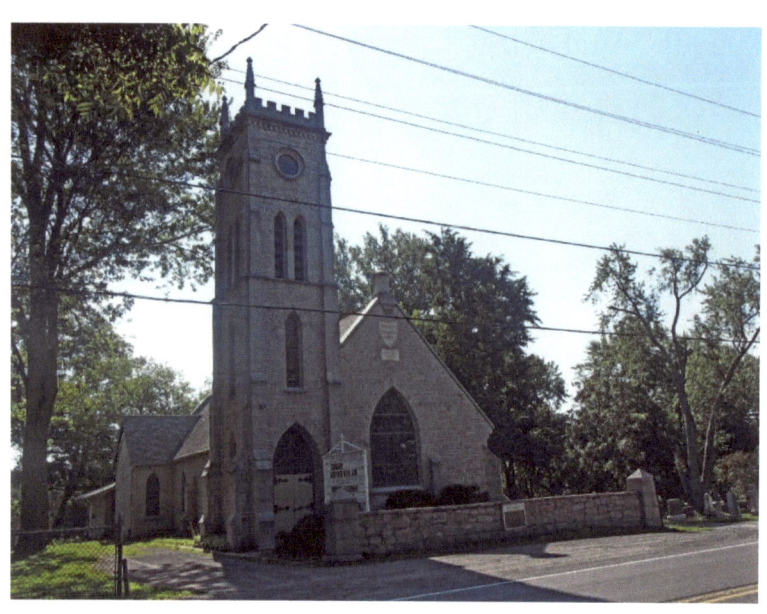

974 Sydenham Road – Christ Church Anglican – 1870 –
Gothic Revival - buttresses, lancet windows, crenelated tower
with finials, dentil moulding

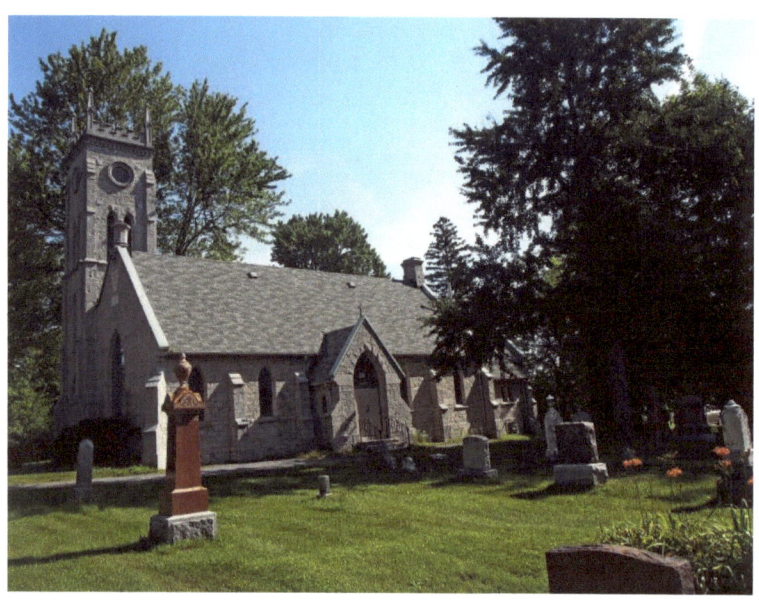

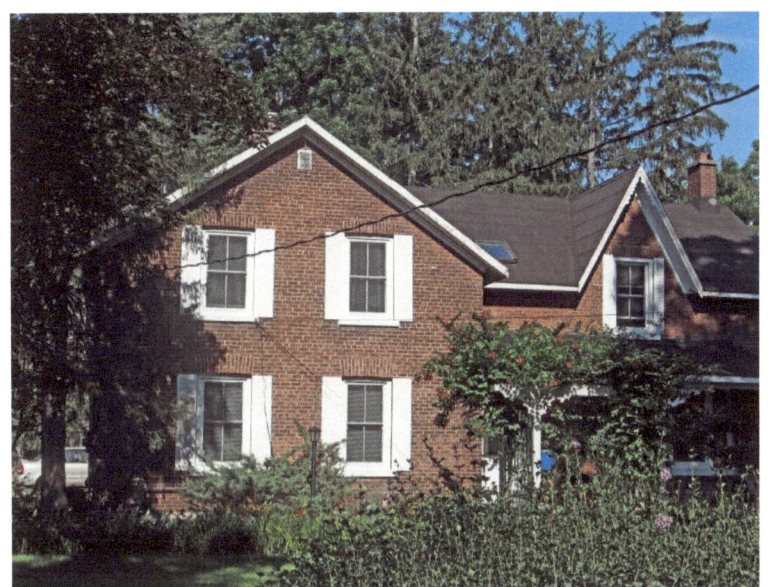

975 Sydenham Road – Gothic Revival

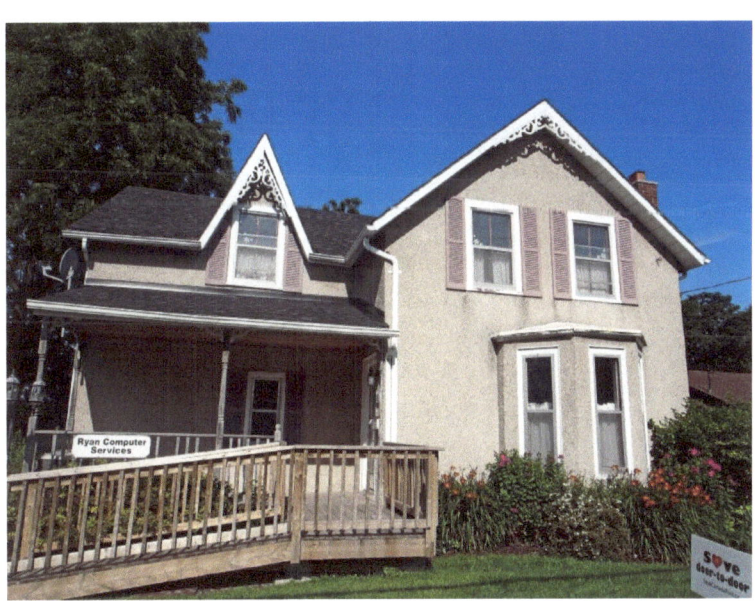

983 Sydenham Road – Gothic Revival, verge board trim on gables, bay window

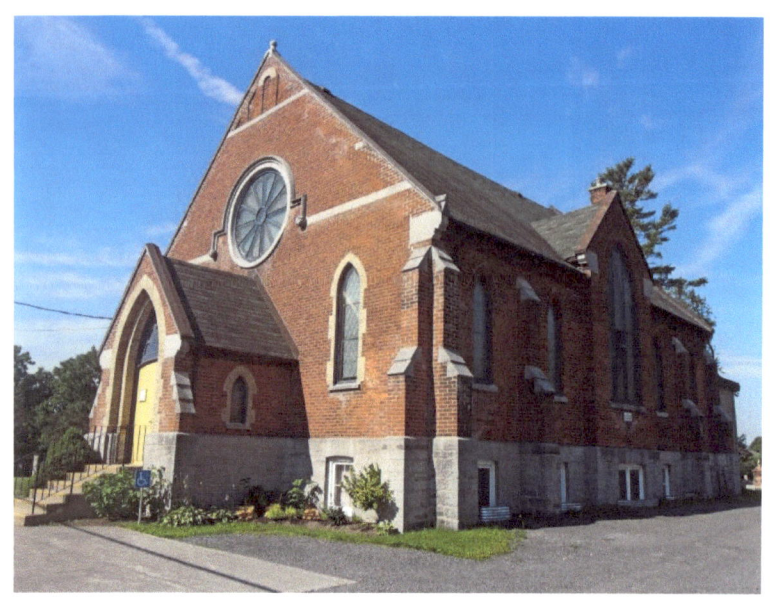

965 Sydenham Road – United Church – buttresses, lancet
windows, rose window

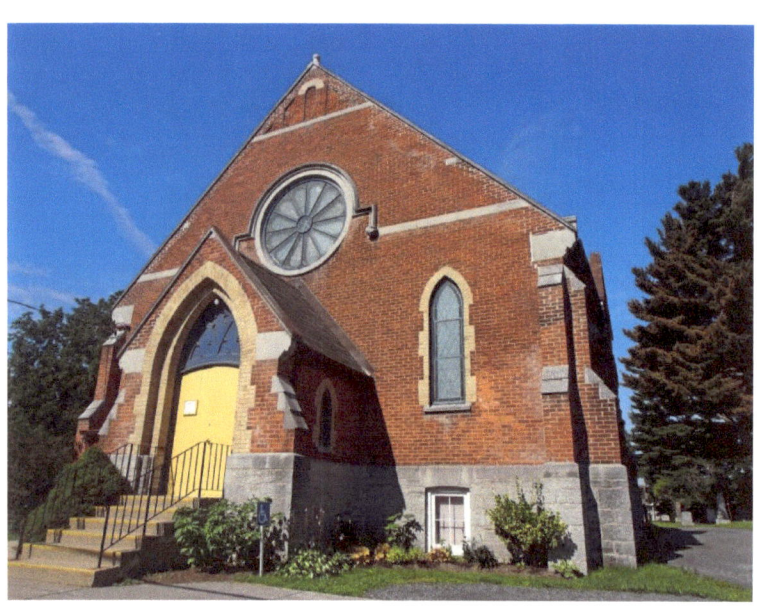

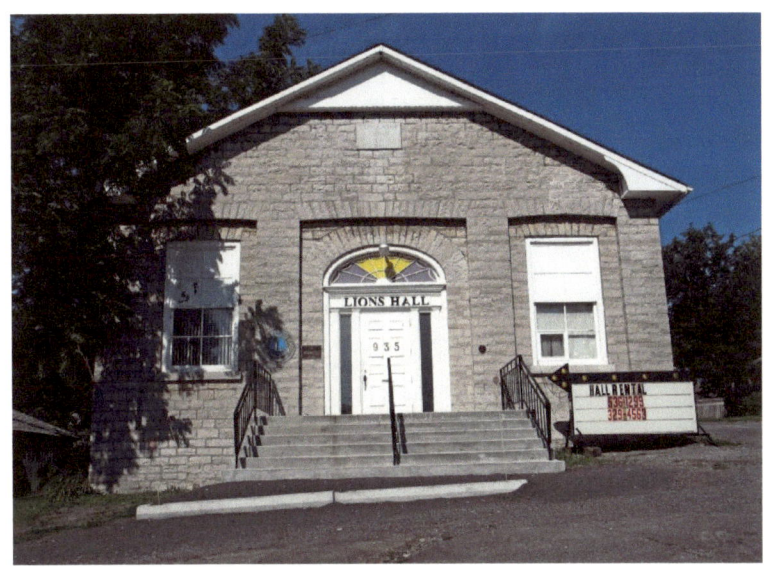

935 Sydenham Road – Lions Hall (Township Hall A.D. 1847)
- limestone

Cavalier Robert de La Salle at Cataraquoi – early in his career, this explorer played a principal role in the expansion of the French fur trade into the Lake Ontario region. In 1673 he arranged a meeting between Governor-General Frontenac, who wanted to shift the fur trade away from Montreal, and representatives of the Iroquois at Cataraquoi, the site of present-day Kingston. Placed in command of Fort Frontenac, the post the governor ordered built here, La Salle soon gained control over trade in the area by acquiring ownership of the establishment as a seigneurial grant. Using the fort as a base, he undertook expeditions to the west and southwest in an attempt to expand his Cataraquoi operation into a vast fur-trading empire.

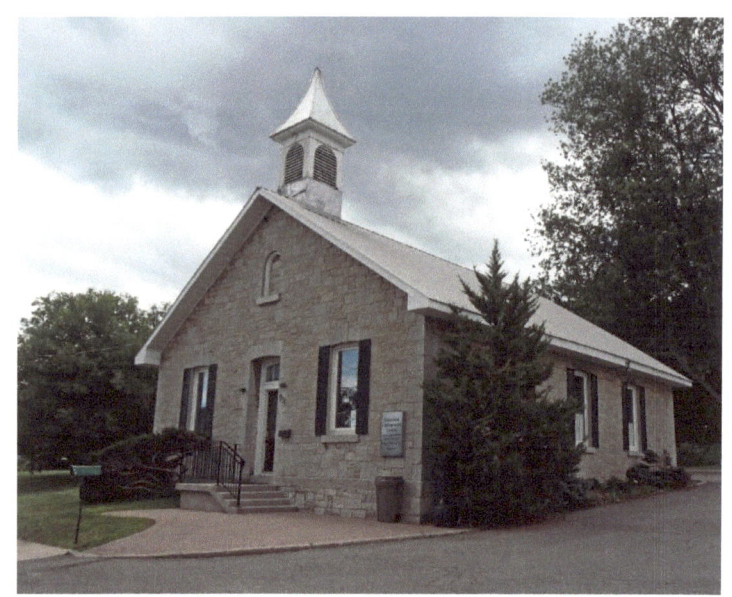

911 Purdy Mills Road - Cataraqui Chiropractic Centre

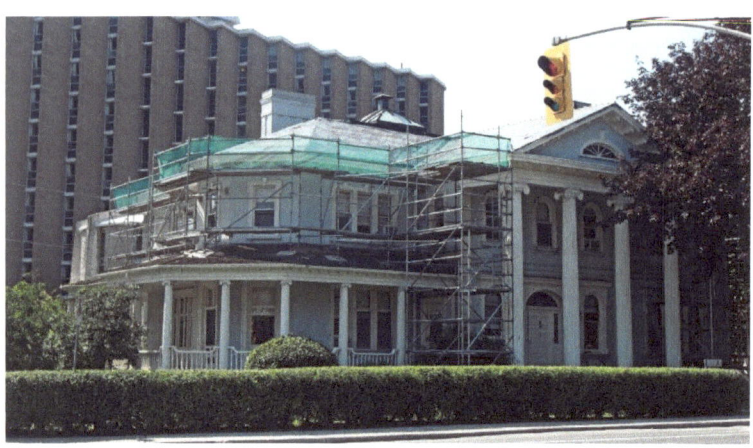

18 Barrie Street – 1830 with alterations between 1862 and 1865 with addition in 1905 of portico with four tall Ionic columns which are repeated on the one-storey side and end verandahs – Classical Revival – pediment with semi-circular window

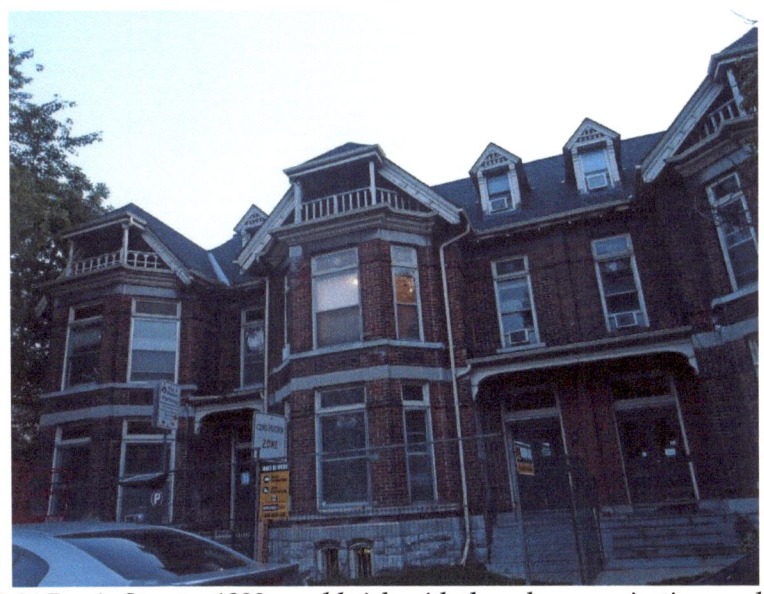

20-24 Barrie Street – 1889 – red brick with three large projecting angled bays two storeys high, topped with sleeping porches with truncated gable roofs, dormers in attic; stone and brick string courses and carved tiles, rectangular transoms in all windows and doors

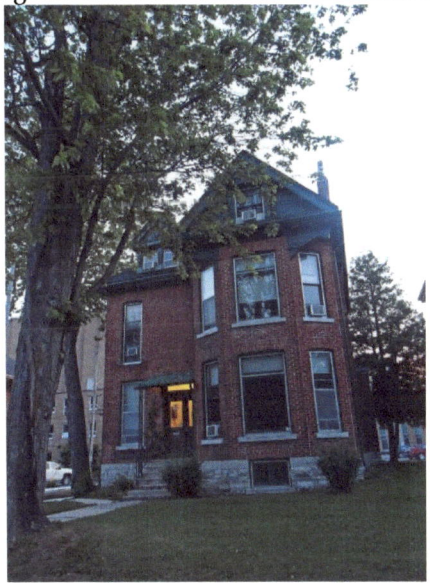

26 Barrie Street – Edwardian, two-storey tower-like bay topped with pediment, dormer

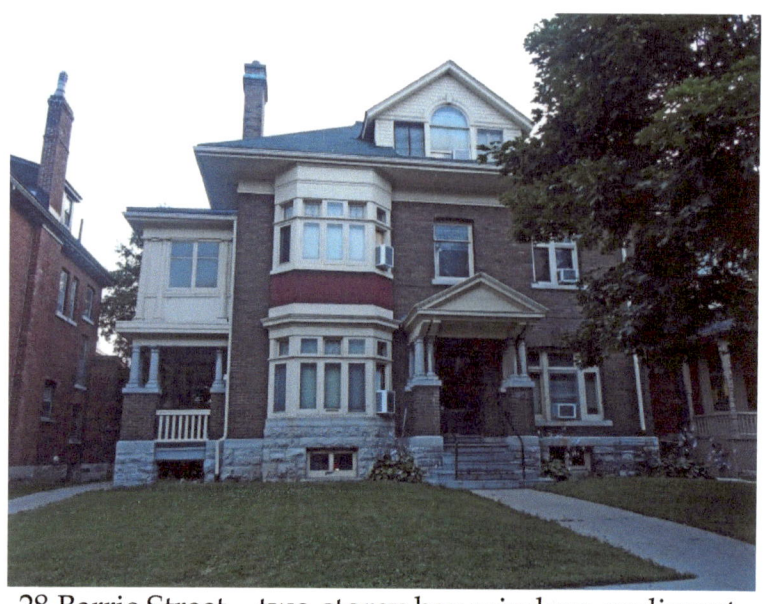

28 Barrie Street – two-storey bay window, pediment, Palladian-type window in dormer

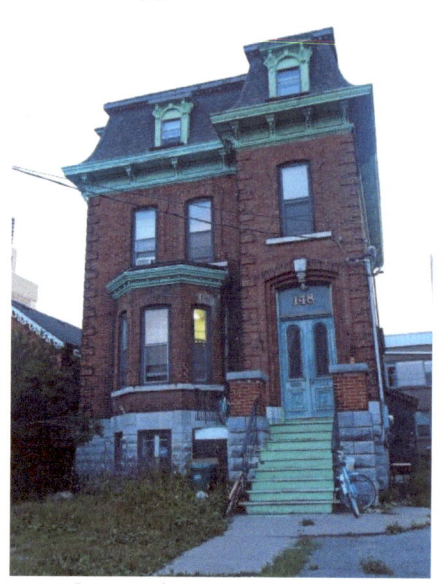

148 Barrie Street – Second Empire – mansard roof, dormers with window hoods, corner quoins, bay window

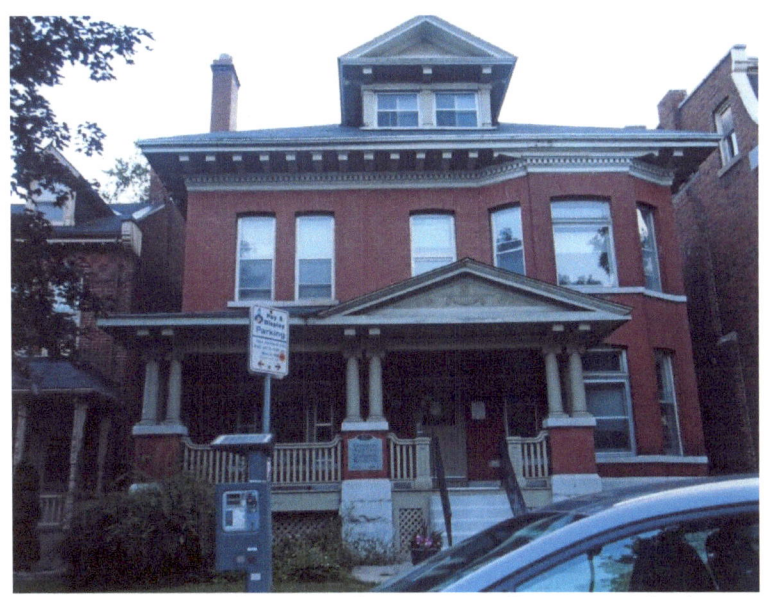

62 Barrie Street – Italianate, dormer, pediment with decorated tympanum, Ionic columns supporting verandah

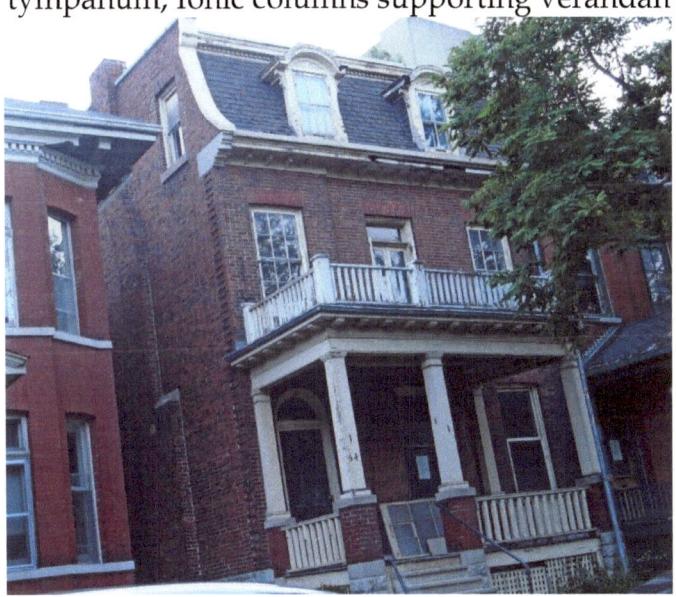

64 Barrie Street – mansard roof with dormers, second floor balcony

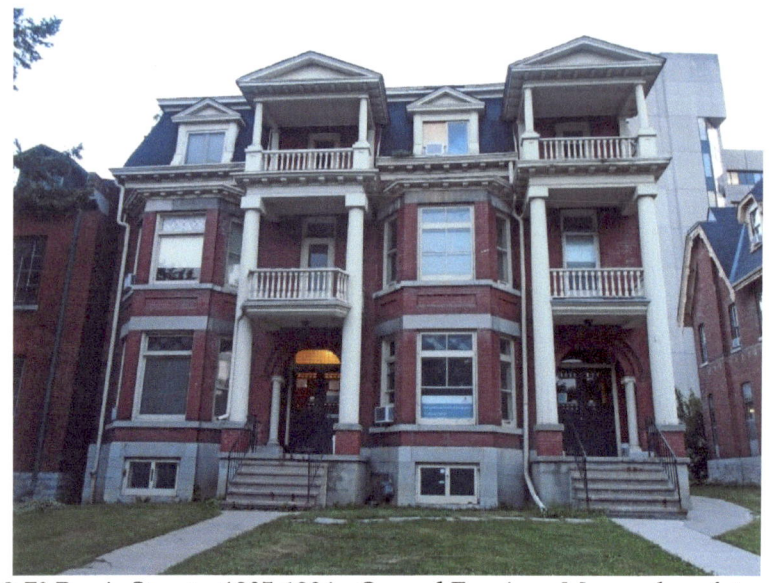

68-70 Barrie Street – 1905-1906 – Second Empire – Mansard roof, two-storey Doric columns with balconies between, third storey sleeping porches with colonettes on the attic balconies topped with pediments, Ionic columns surrounding doors, transom windows

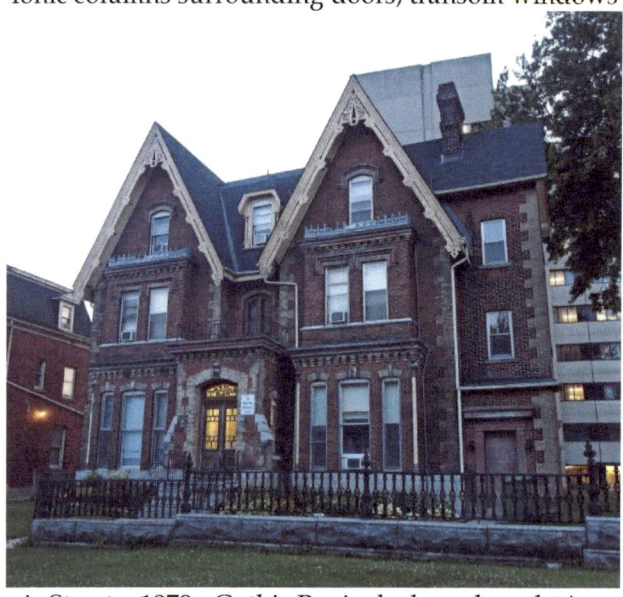

72-74 Barrie Street – 1879 - Gothic Revival – bargeboard trim on gables, iron cresting above two-storey bay windows, corner quoins, second floor balcony, bevelled dentil moulding

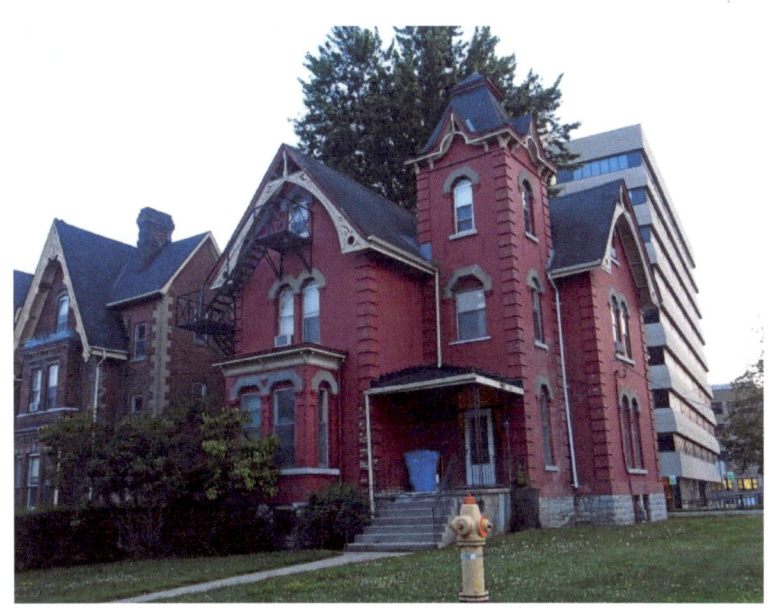

78 Barrie Street – Queen Anne style – three storey tower, cornice brackets, corner quoins, verge board trim on gables

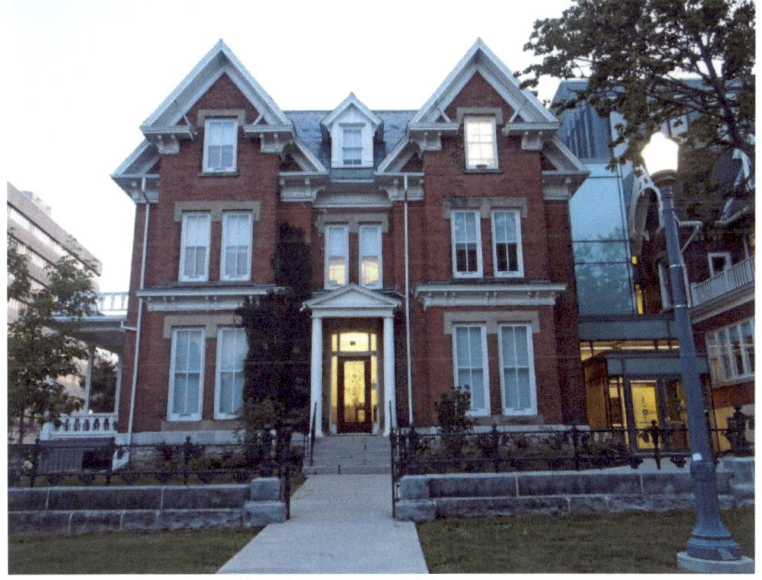

80 Barrie Street – Italianate – 2½-storey tower-like bays, cornice return on gables, dormer between gables, cornice brackets, pediment above door, sidelights and transom

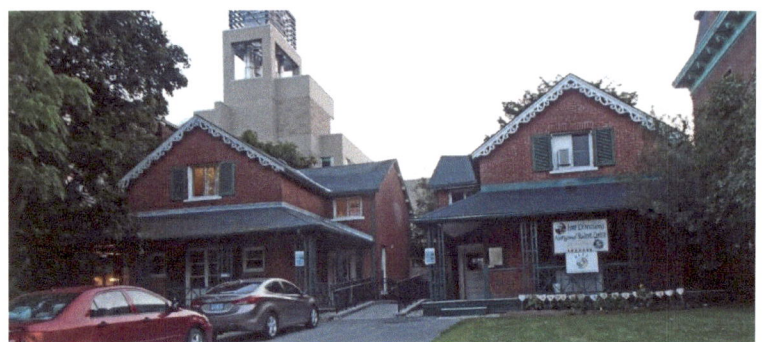

Barrie Street - Gothic Revival – verge board trim on gables

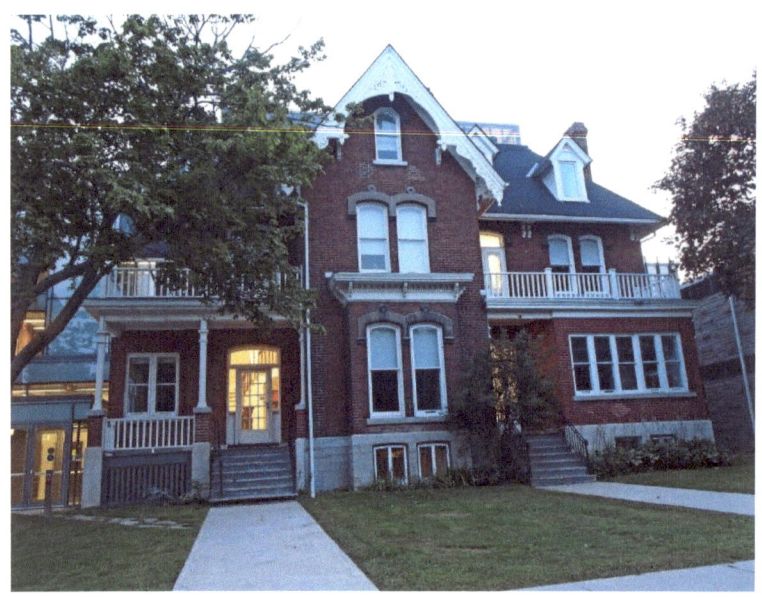

82 Barrie Street – verge board trim on gable, bay window,
second floor balconies, dormer in attic of wing

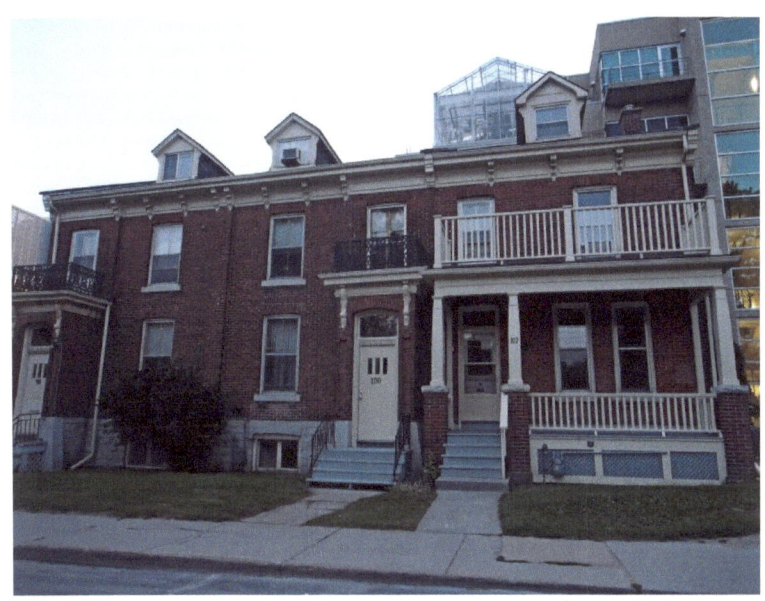

98-102 Barrie Street – dormers – second floor balconies, transom windows

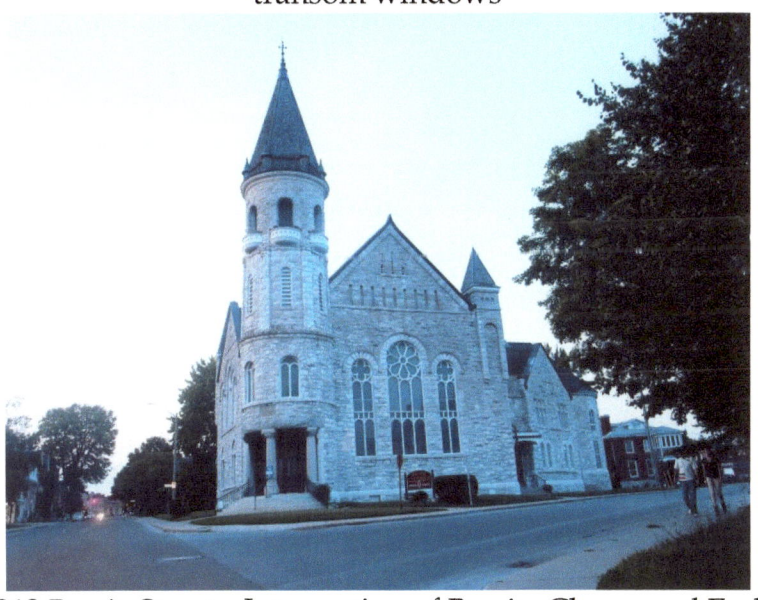

212 Barrie Street - Intersection of Barrie, Clergy and Earl Streets - Chalmers United Church – 1890 – Romanesque style, rose windows, quatrefoils, rounded tower, columns with Corinthian capitals

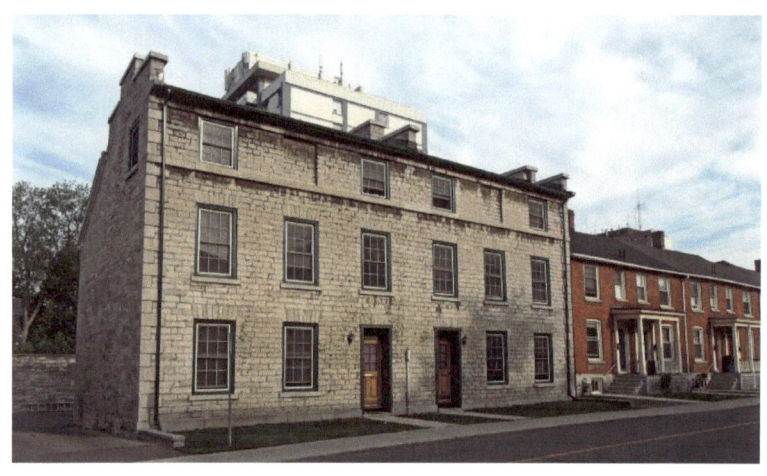

286-288 Barrie Street – limestone, voussoirs, corner quoins

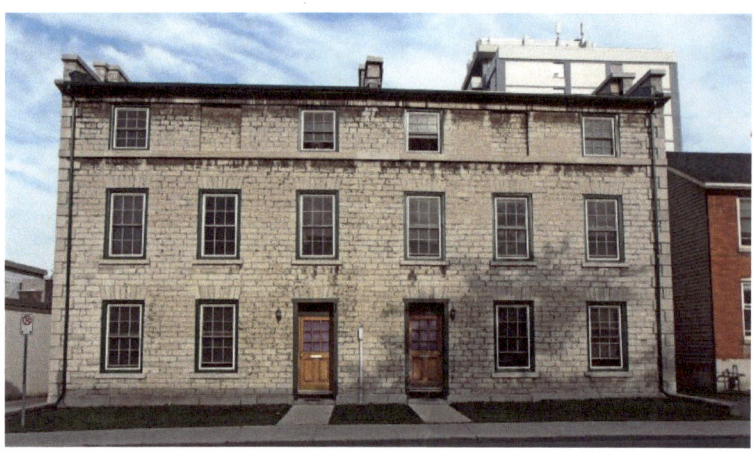

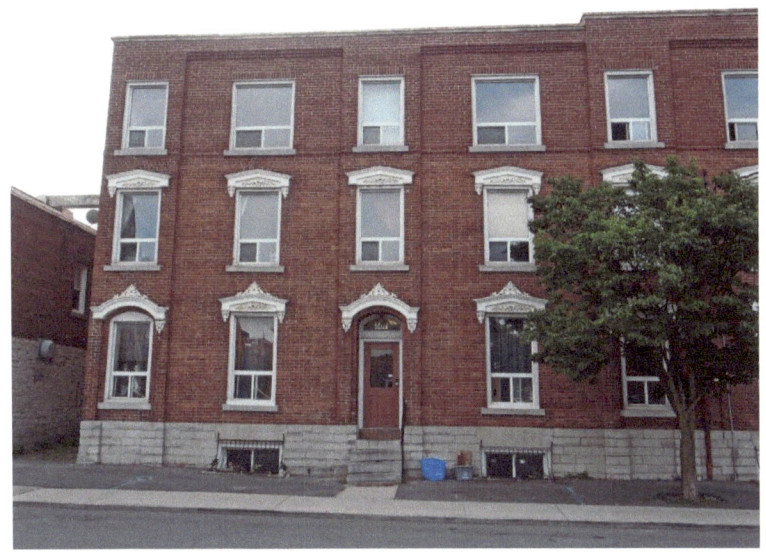

307 Barrie Street – window hoods on first two storeys

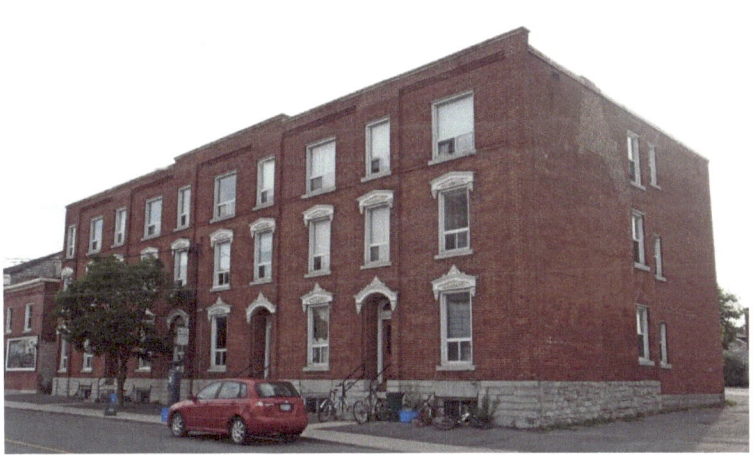

Barrie Street

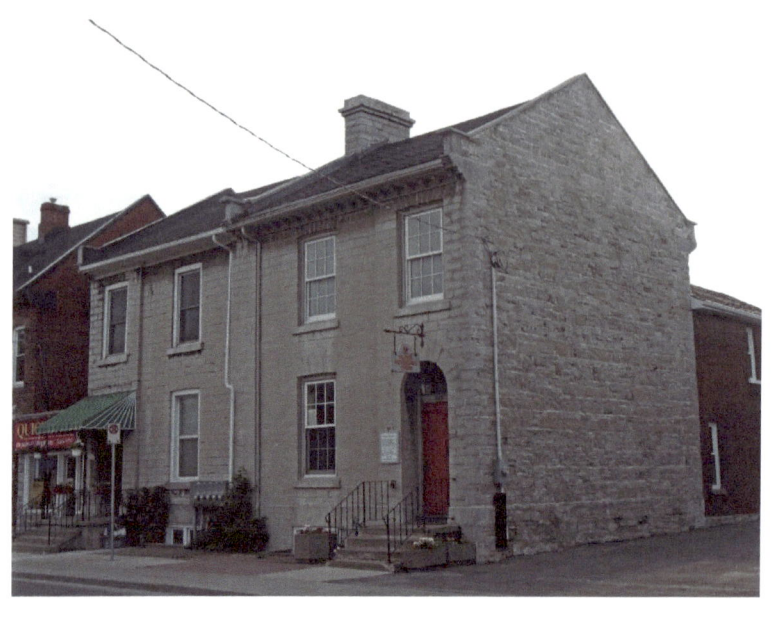

327-329 Barrie Street – limestone, cornice brackets,
six-over-six window panes

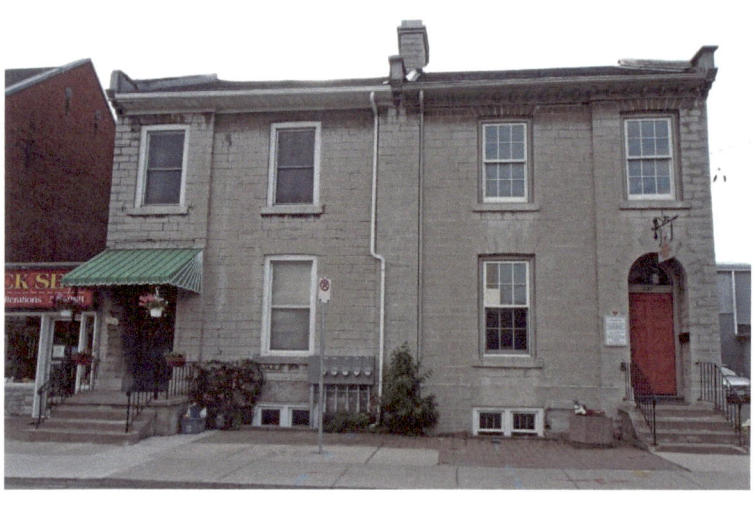

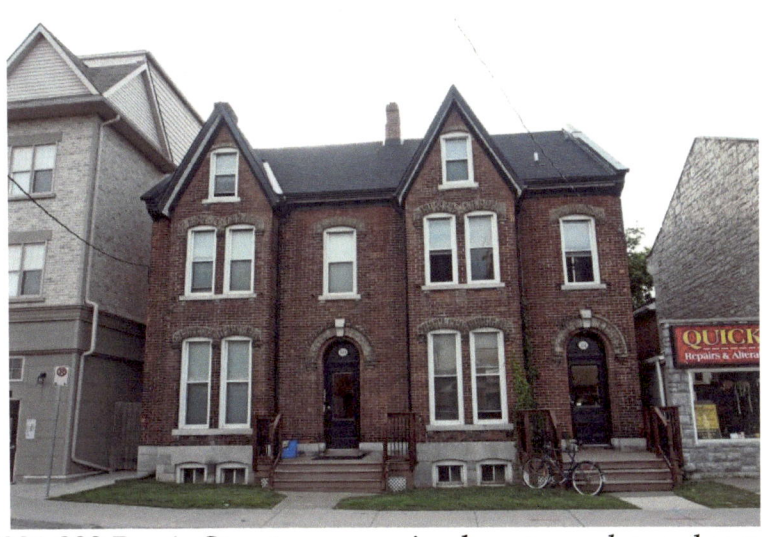

331-333 Barrie Street – voussoirs, keystone above doors,
2½ storey frontispiece on each side

Barriefield Village

In 1814, Richard Cartwright created a town site on his property near the Naval Shipyards, and the first building lots were sold in June of 1814 to officers, armorers, boat builders, butchers, carpenters, coopers and stone masons from the nearby Naval Dockyard and Fort Henry. Named after the commissioner of the Kingston Naval Dockyard, Commodore Sir Robert Barrie, Barriefield Village prospered for many decades, with an important boatbuilding industry on the waterfront. Barriefield Village sits on a high embankment on the eastern shore of the Great Cataraqui River near the intersection of Highways 2 and 15, adjacent to Fort Henry and CFB Kingston. This quaint village has a distinctive building style typically consisting of low profile, one-and-a-half storey homes of wood frame or stone construction. Most of the buildings are single detached residences with a few semi-detached or row-type houses.

In the mid-twentieth century, the economic life of the village declined, but the nineteenth century village was largely preserved. In 1980, Barriefield became the first village in Ontario to be designated a Heritage Conservation District.

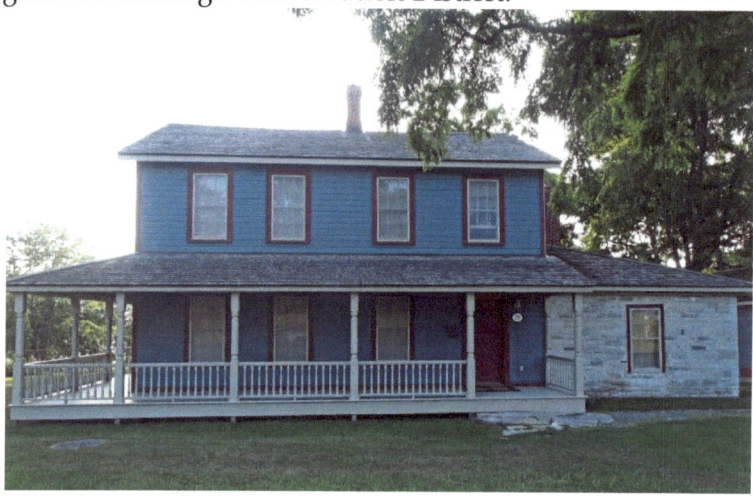

275 Main Street – John Mark's house - two storey wood frame, one storey stone

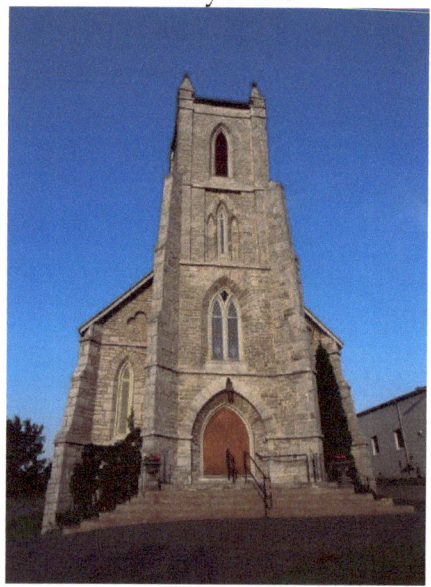

268 Main Street - St. Mark's Anglican Church – corner stone laid July 10, 1843, opened July 7, 1844 – early Gothic Revival style

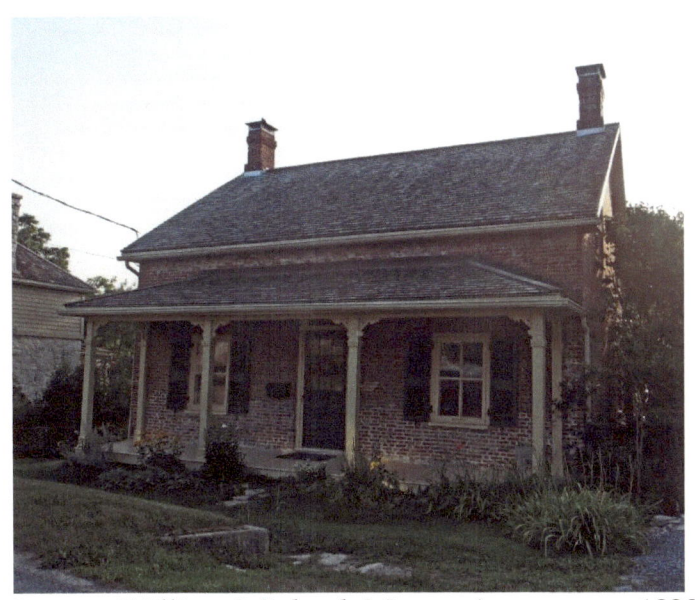

Main Street – William Michael, Master Armourer – 1820 – 1½ storey brick

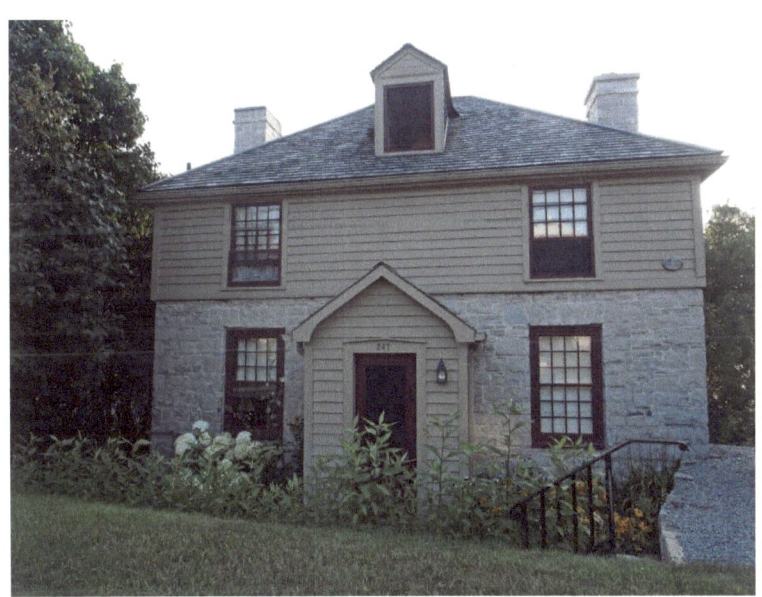

247 Main Street – one storey stone, second storey addition – 12-over-12 window panes; dormer in attic of hipped roof

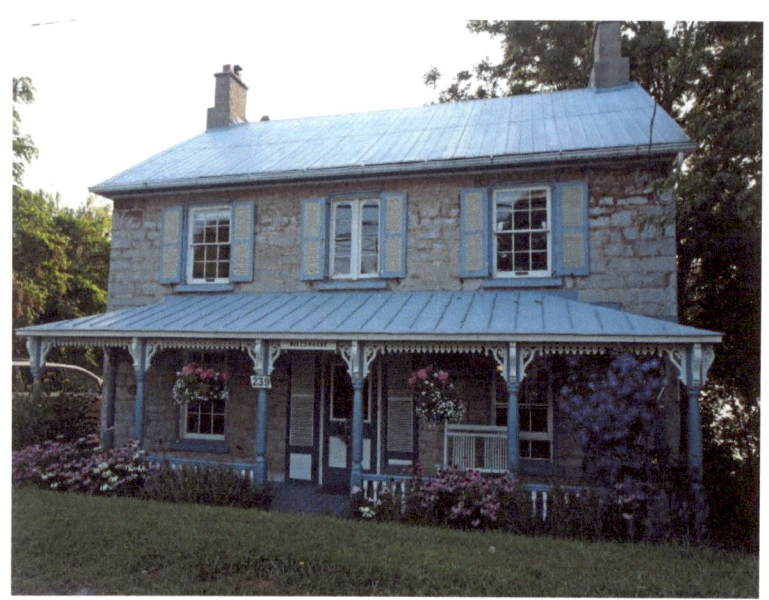

239 Main Street – Willowmere - two-storey limestone, 6-over-6 window panes, turned wooden posts for verandah support with bric-a-brac trim

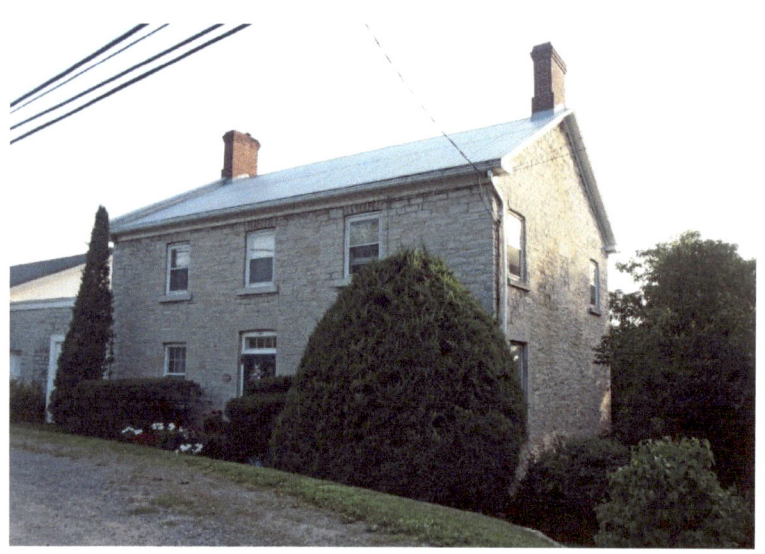

233 Main Street – two-storey limestone

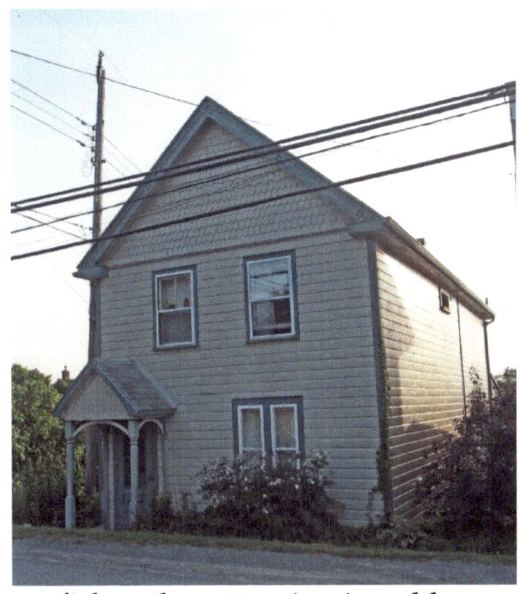

Main Street – fish scale patterning in gable, cornice return

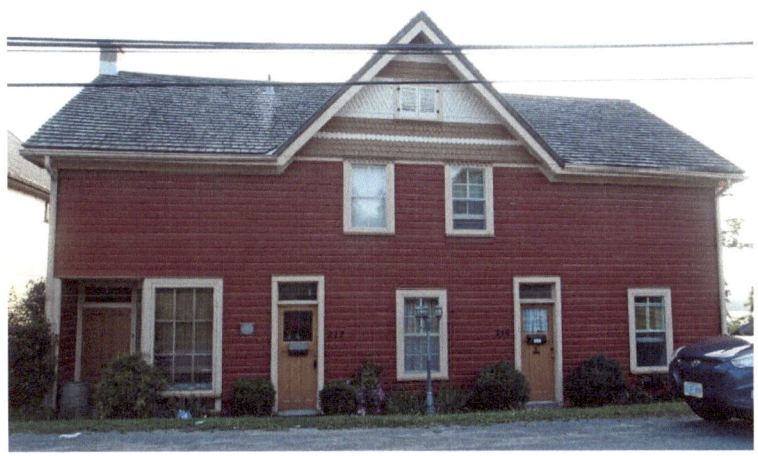

217-219 Main Street – built in the late 19th century – the south end of the building was a store into the 1960s – wood frame, fish scale and other patterning in gable

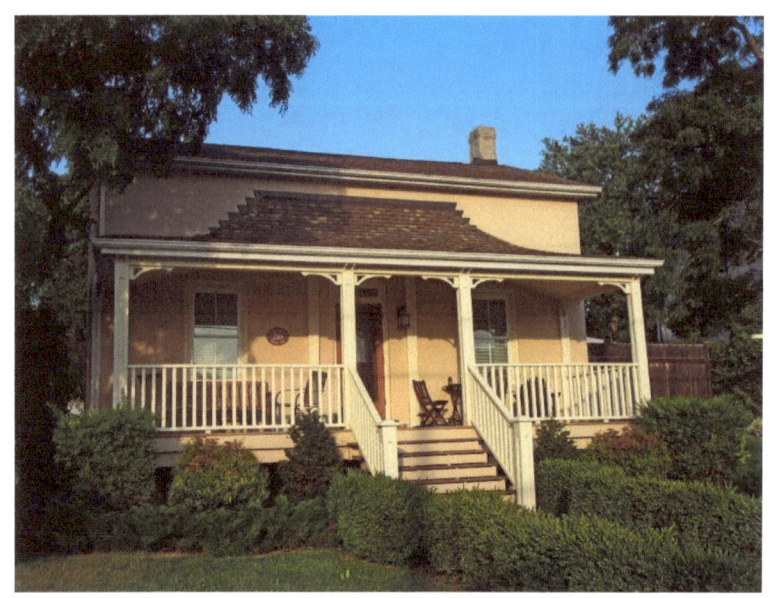

210 Main Street – George Medley House - 1867

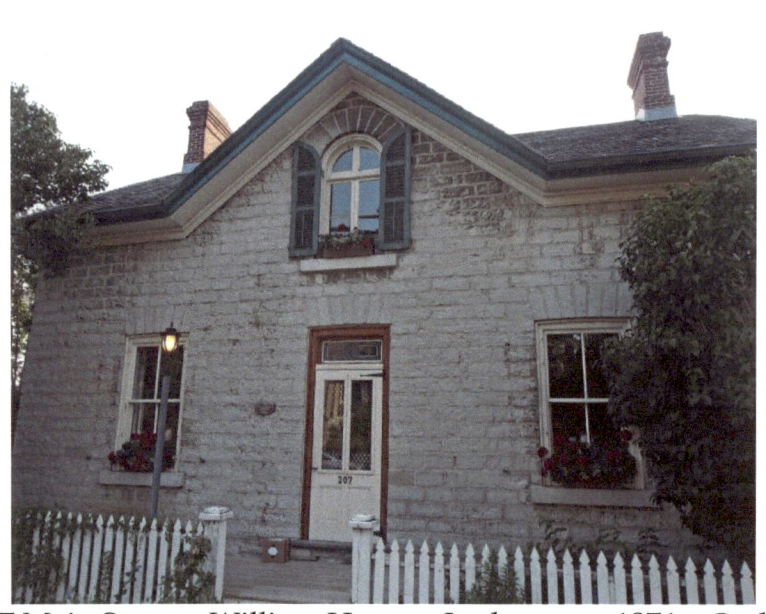

207 Main Street – William Hutton, Innkeeper – 1874 – Gothic Revival - 1½ storey stone, semi-circular window in gable

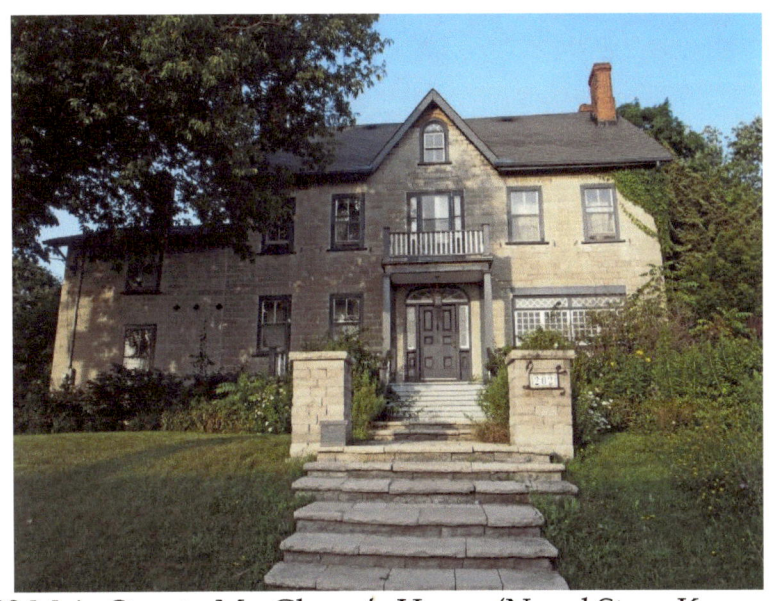

202 Main Street - Mr. Glover's House (Naval Store Keeper) -
1845 – known as Barriefield House

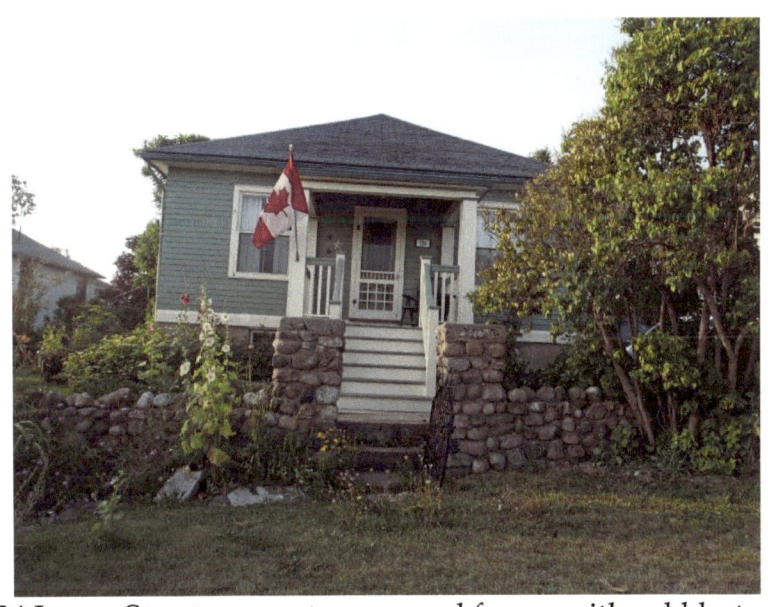

234 James Street – one-storey wood frame with cobblestone
pillars and wall

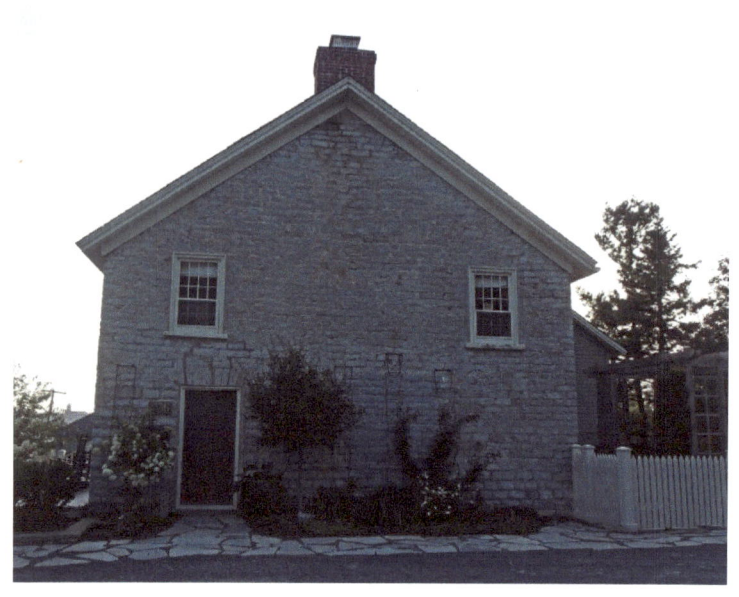

236 James Street – two-storey limestone, 12-over-12, and 8-over-8 window panes, transom window above door

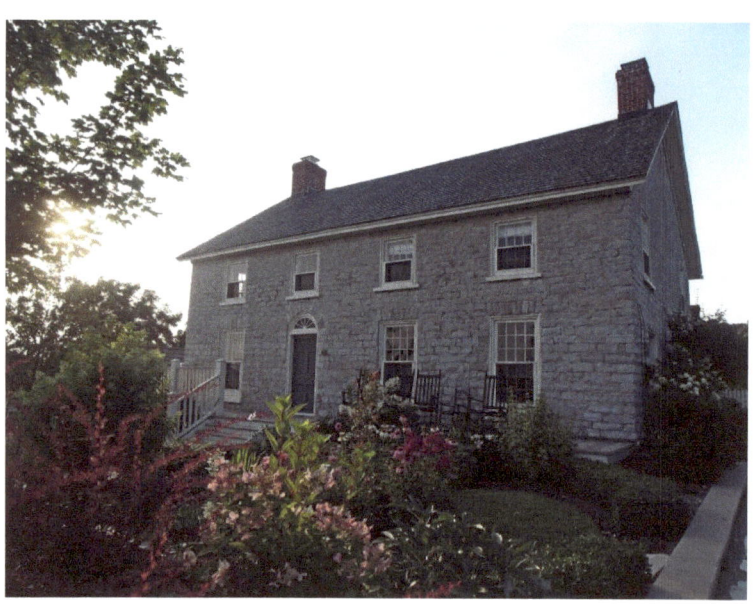

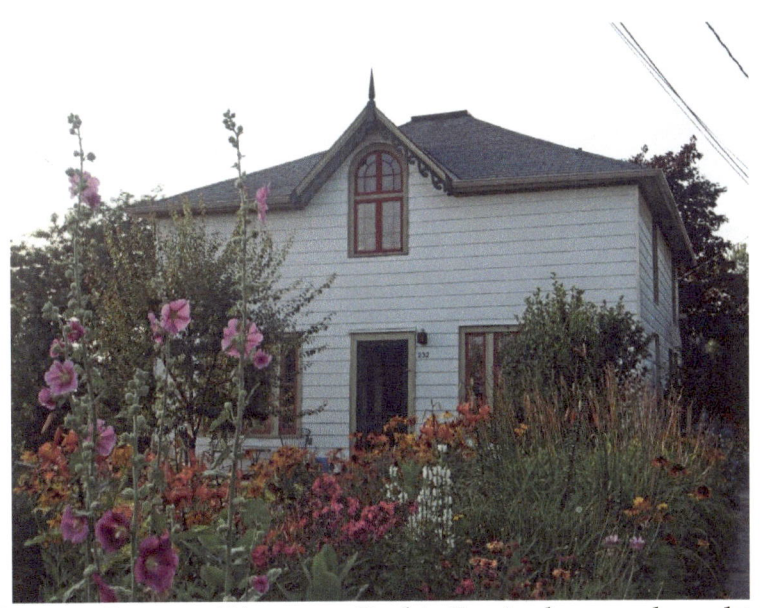

232 James Street – 1½ storey Gothic Revival, verge board trim and finial on gable with semi-circular window

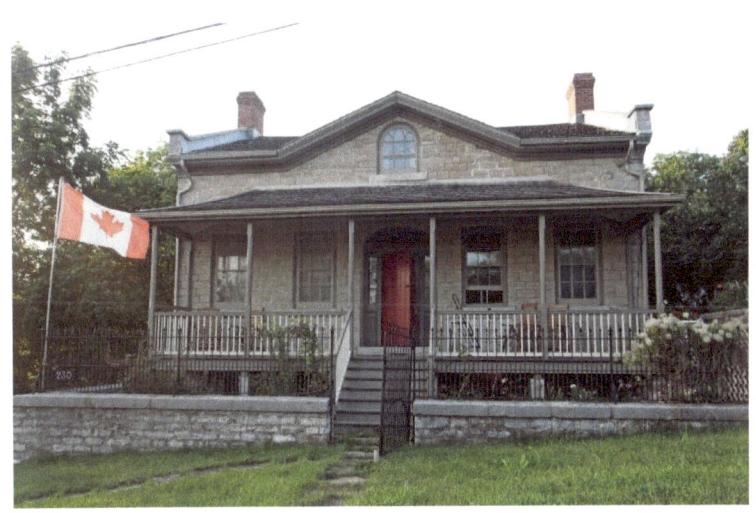

Sharman's Lane – 1½ storey limestone, 6-over-6 window panes, sidelights and transom surrounding door

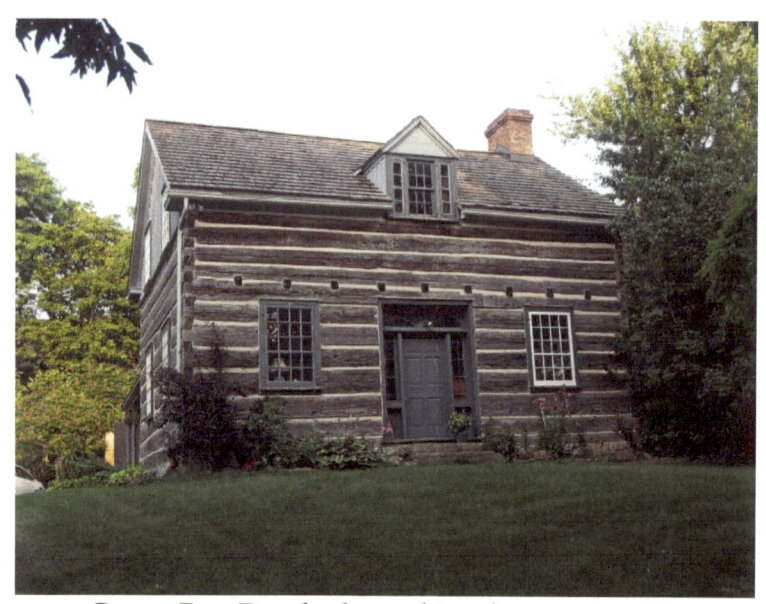

Green Bay Road – log cabin, dormer in attic

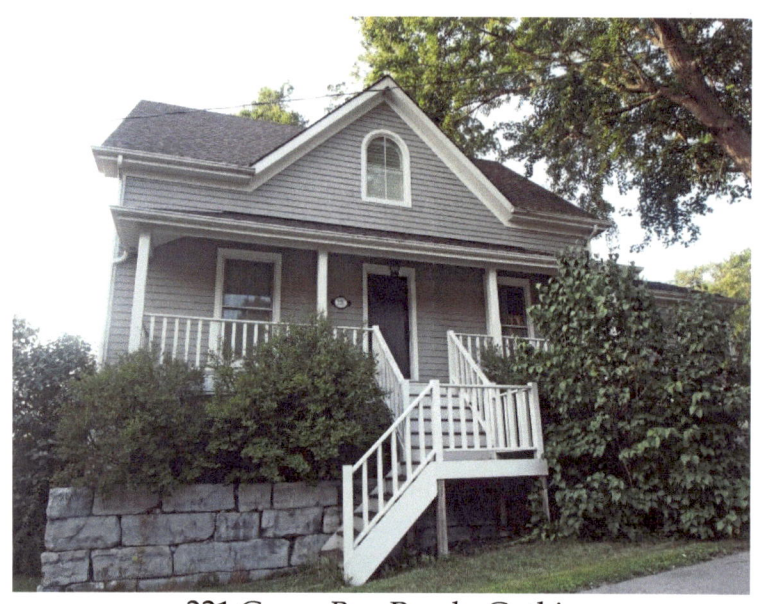

221 Green Bay Road - Gothic

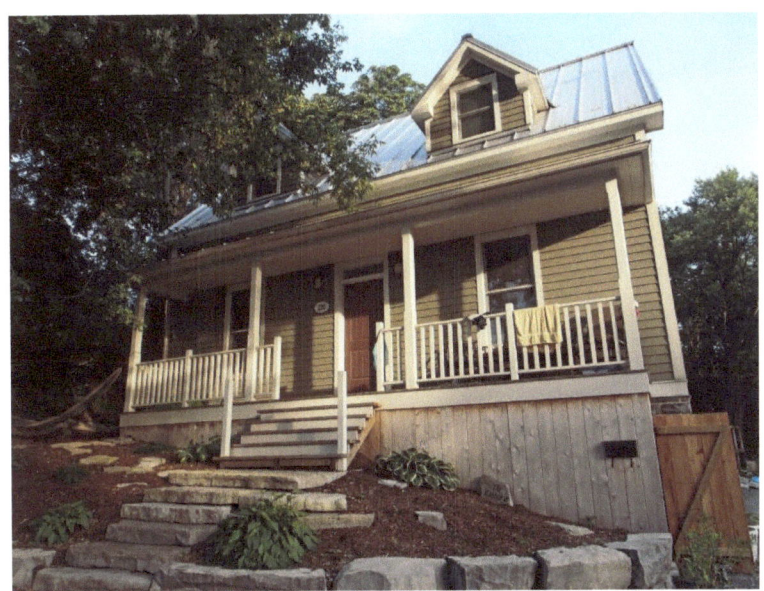

220 Green Bay Road – dormers in attic

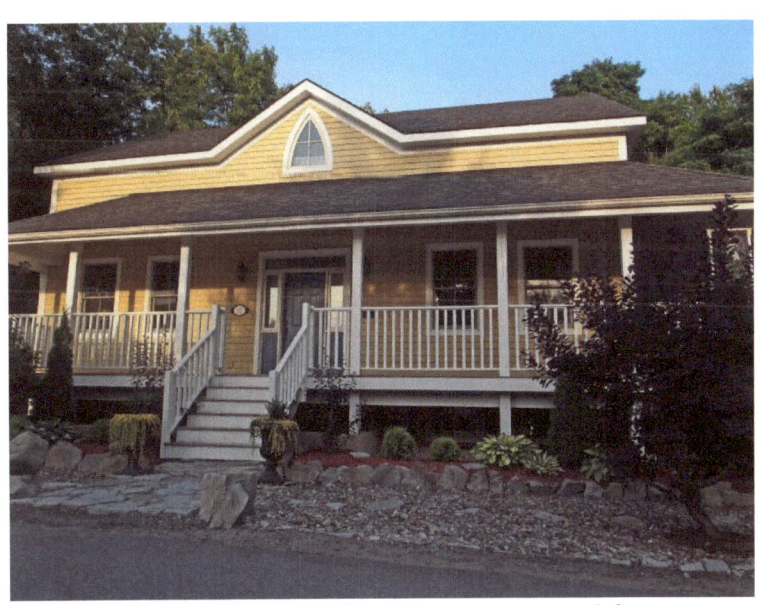

222 Green Bay Road – 1½ storey wood frame

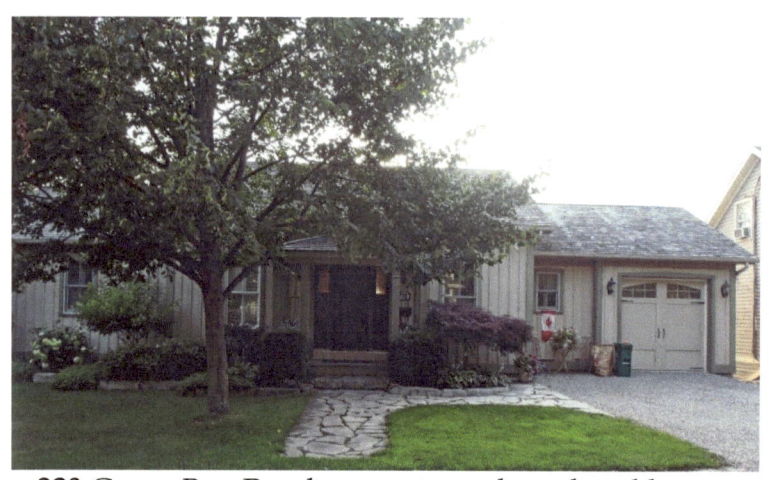

223 Green Bay Road – one storey board and batten

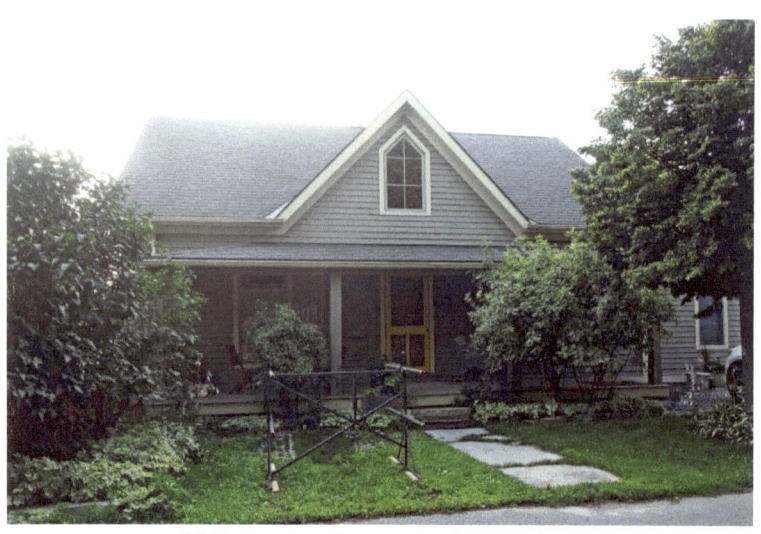

225 Green Bay Road - Gothic

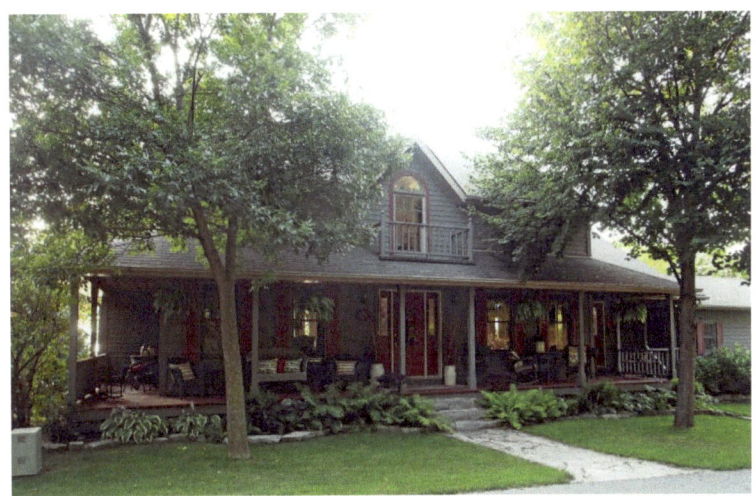

227 Green Bay Road – Gothic, second floor balcony, sidelights

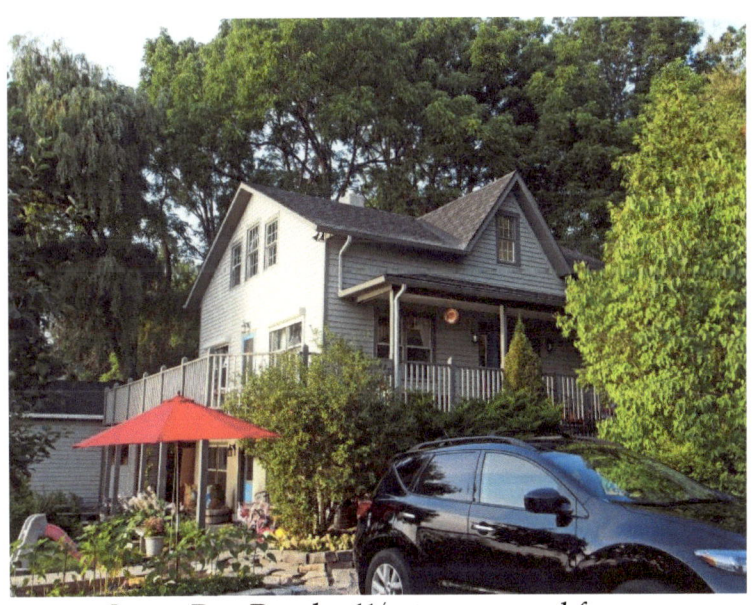

Green Bay Road – 1½ storey wood frame

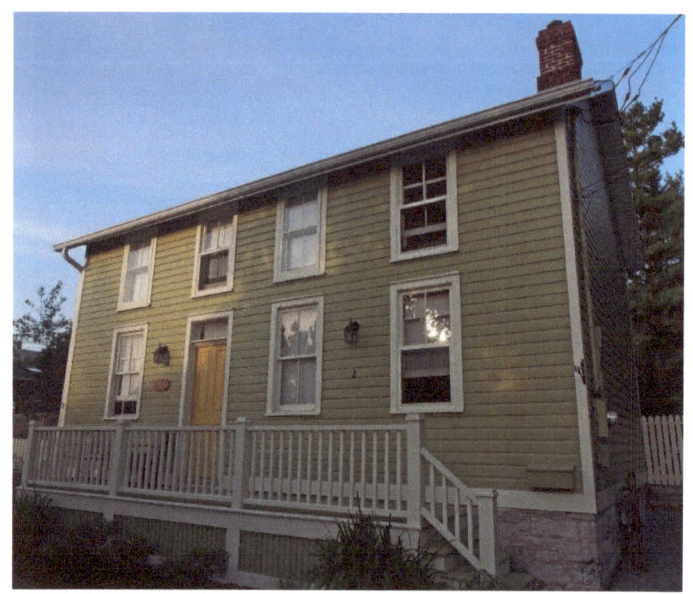

2 Sharman's Lane – two storey wood frame

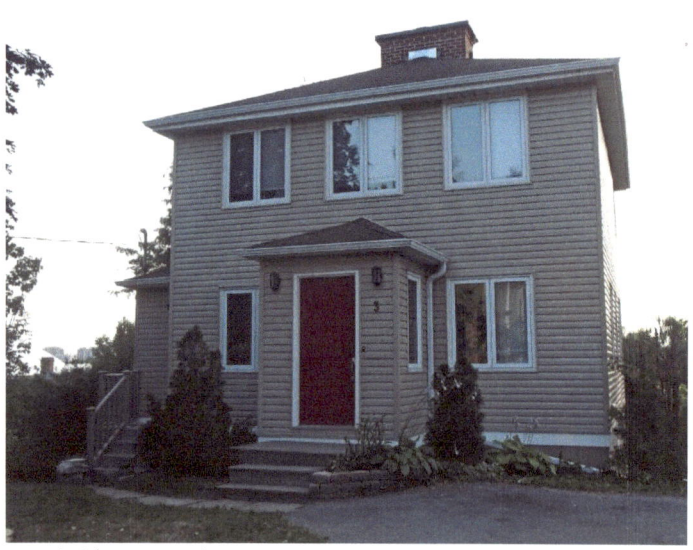

3 Sharman's Lane – two storey wood frame

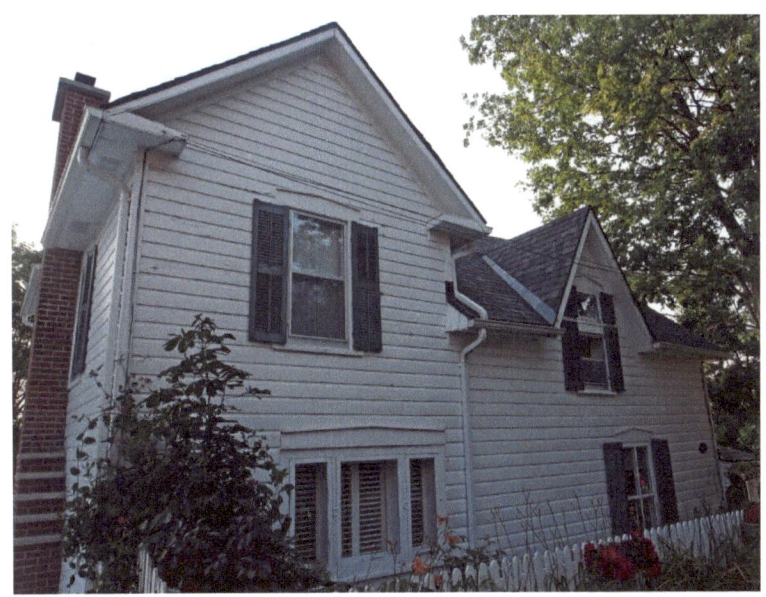

Sharman's Lane – Gothic Revival - 1½ storey wood frame, cornice return on gable

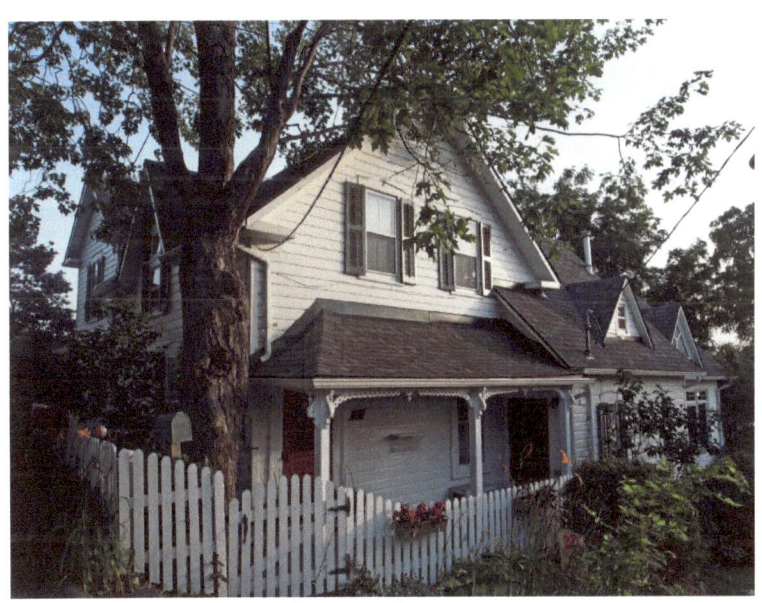

Sharman's Lane

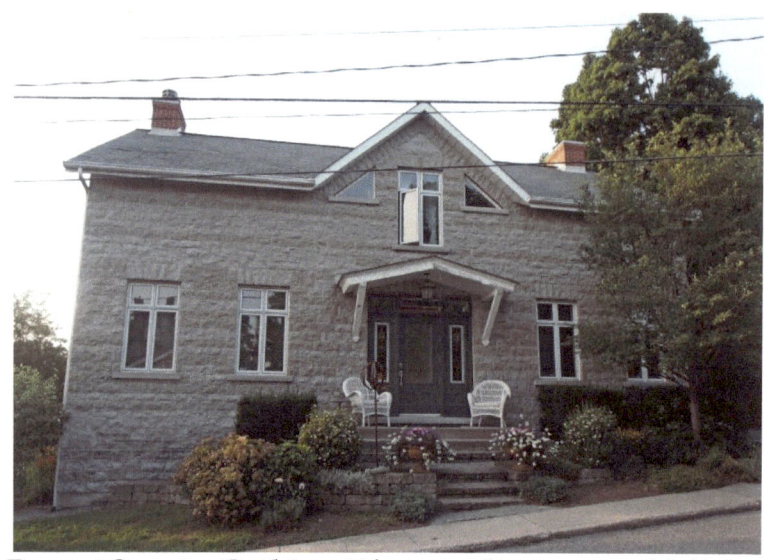

Regent Street – Gothic – 1½ storey limestone, sidelights

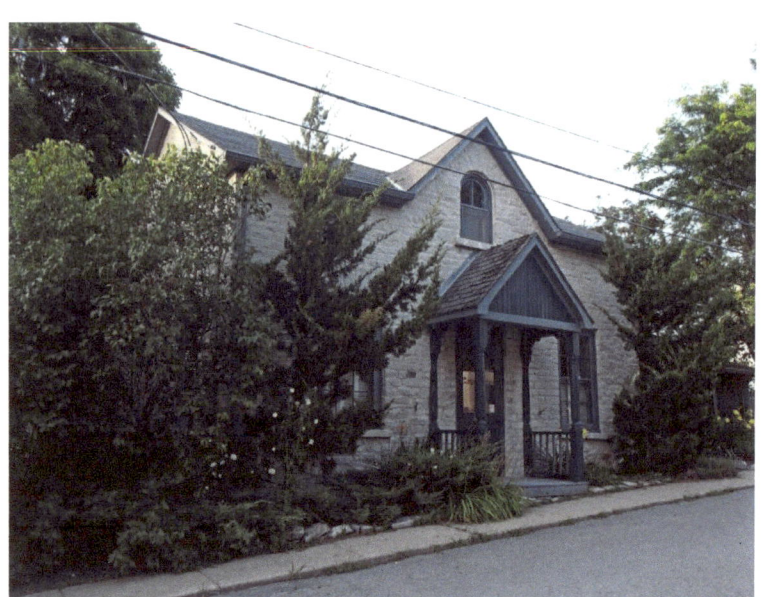

407 Regent Street – Robert Forbes House – 1854 - 1½ storey
limestone, semi-circular window in gable

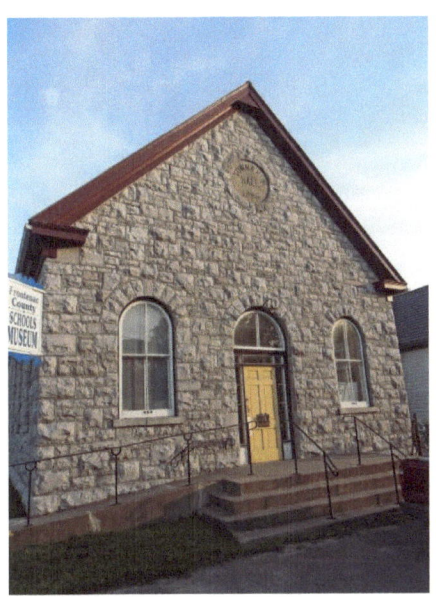

Regent Street – Frontenac County Museum - Township Hall –
1886 – limestone, semi-circular windows

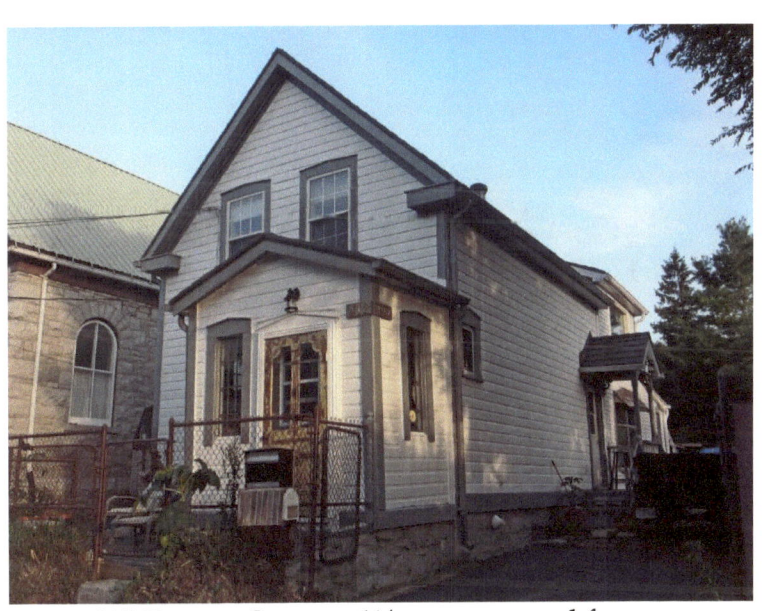

412 Regent Street – 1½ storey wood frame,
cornice return on gable

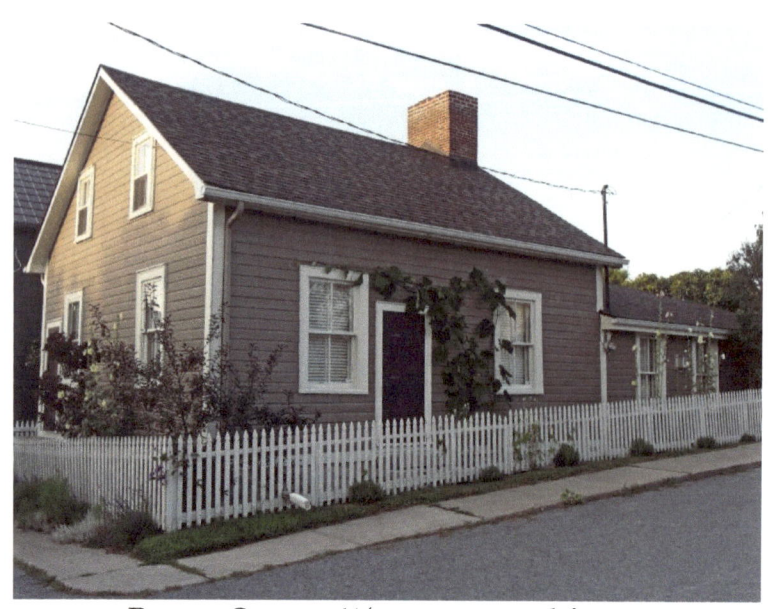

Regent Street - 1½ storey wood frame

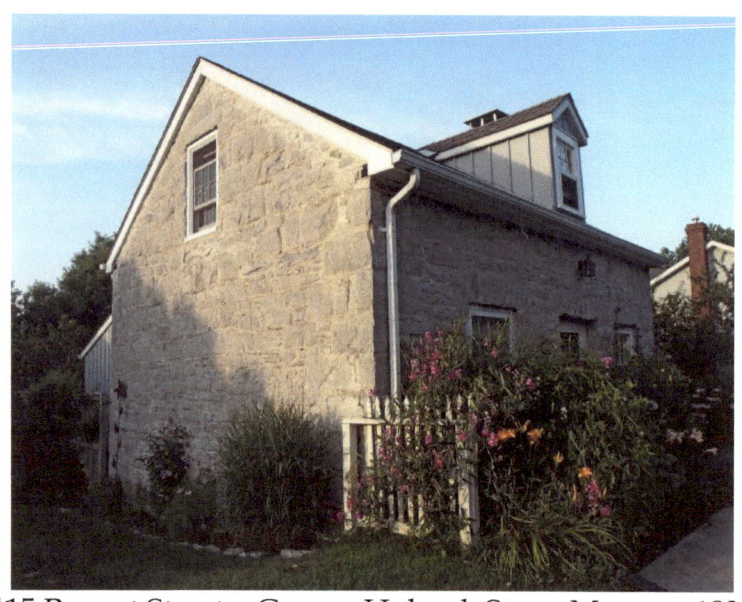

415 Regent Street – George Hyland, Stone Mason – 1830
– 1½ storey limestone, dormer in attic

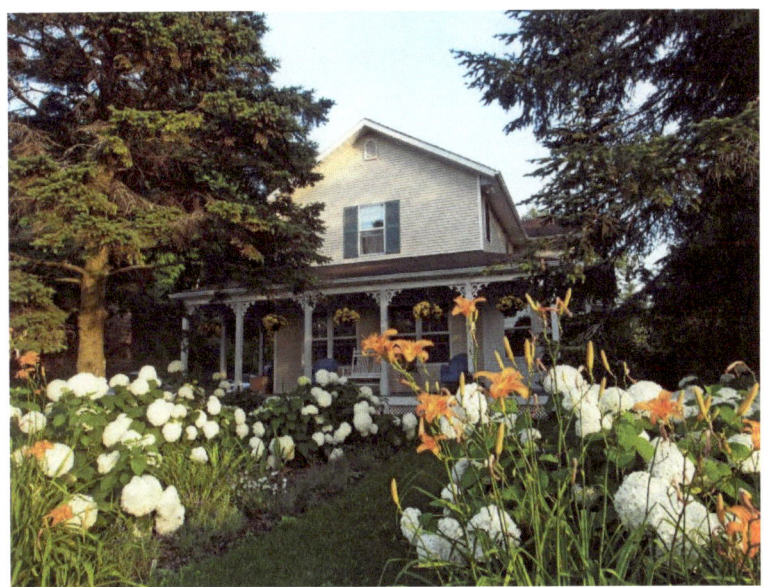

Regent Street – bric-a-brac on verandah

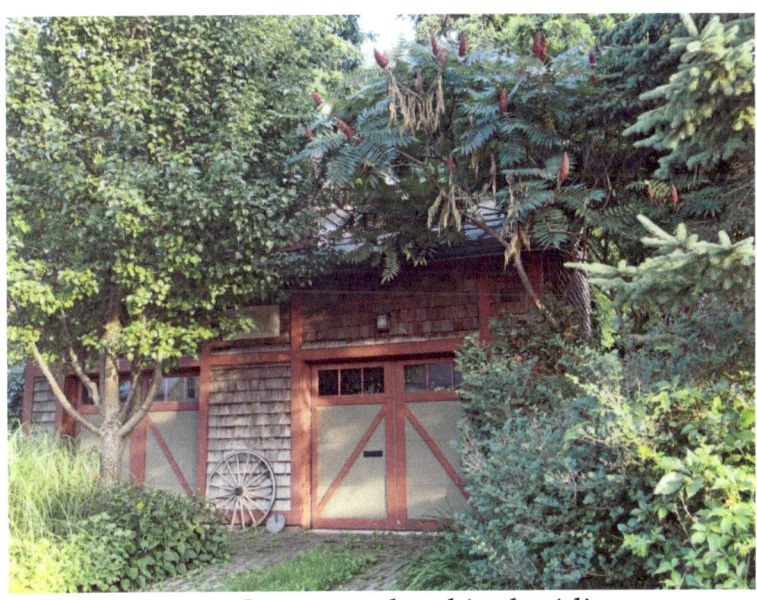

Regent Street – cedar shingle siding

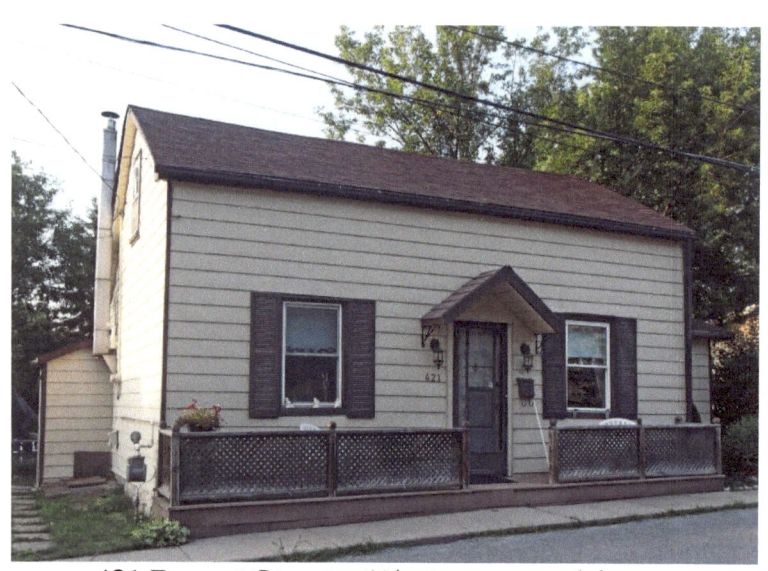

421 Regent Street – 1½ storey wood frame

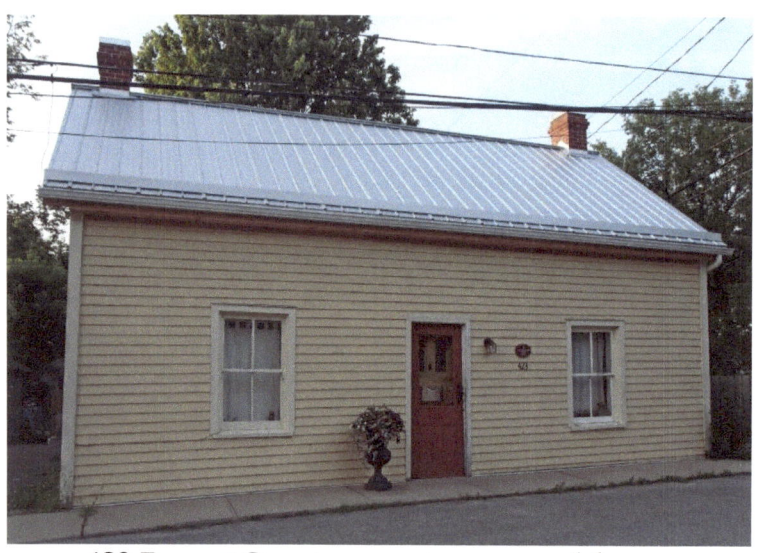

423 Regent Street – one storey wood frame

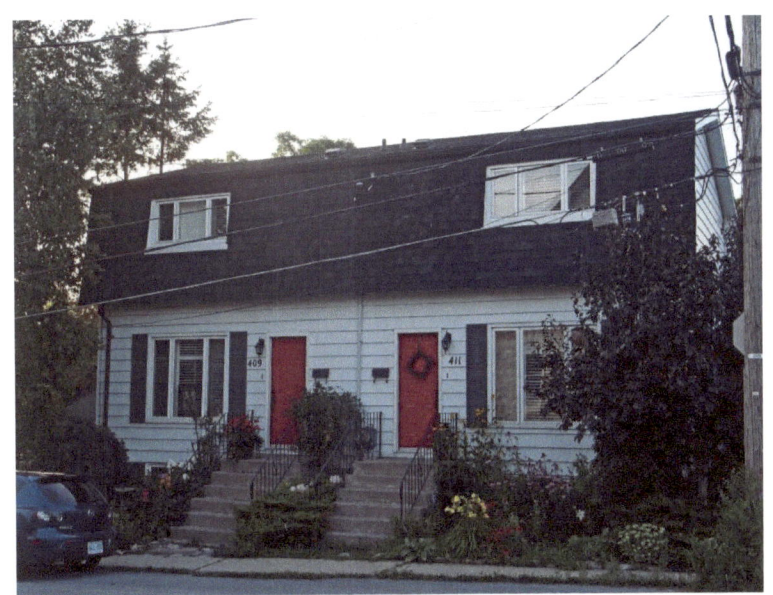

409-411 Regent Street

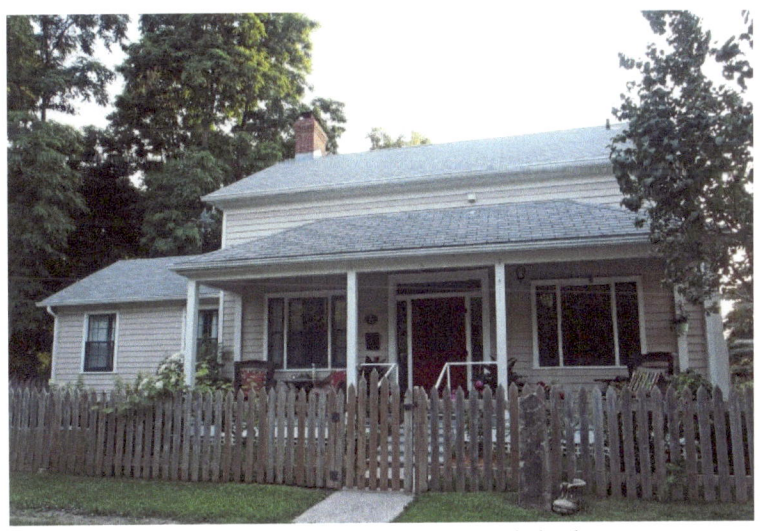

3 George Street – 1885 - sidelights

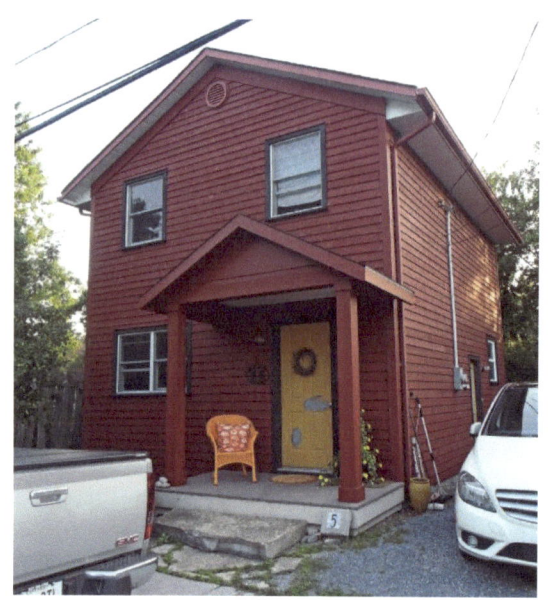

5 George Street – 1½ storey wood frame

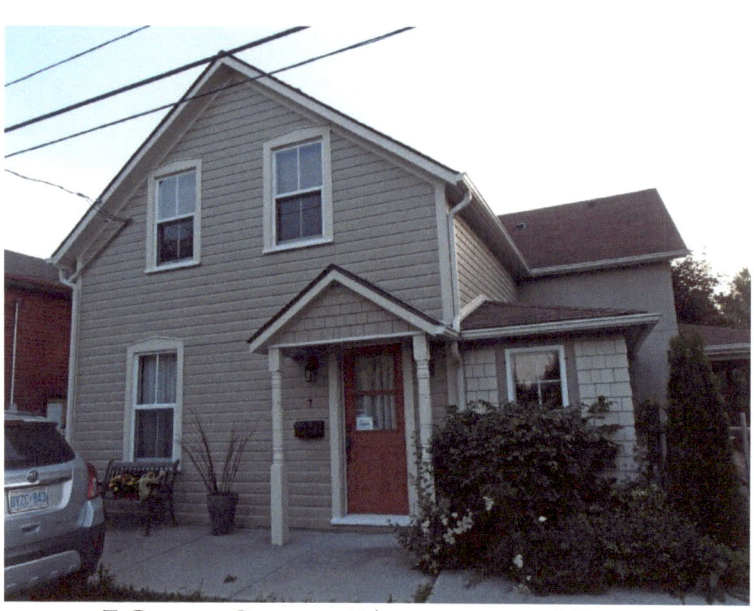

7 George Street – 1½ storey wood frame

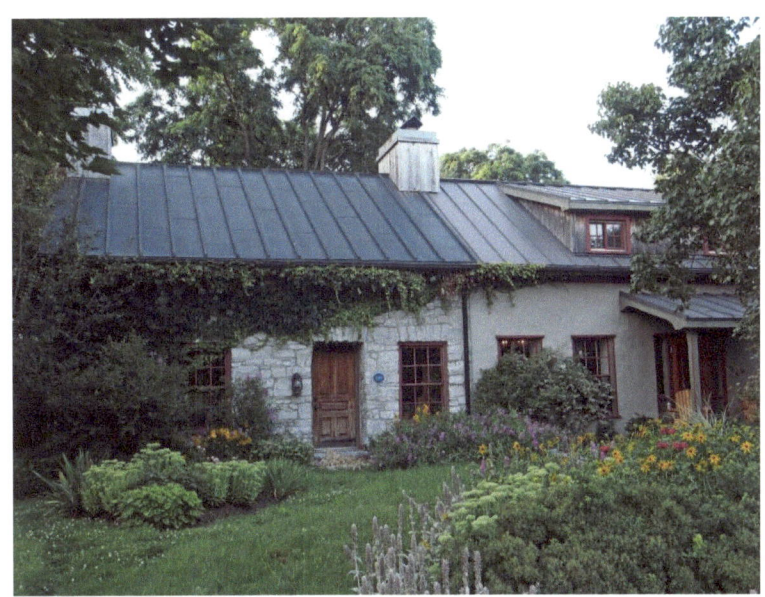

246 James Street – one storey stone, dormers

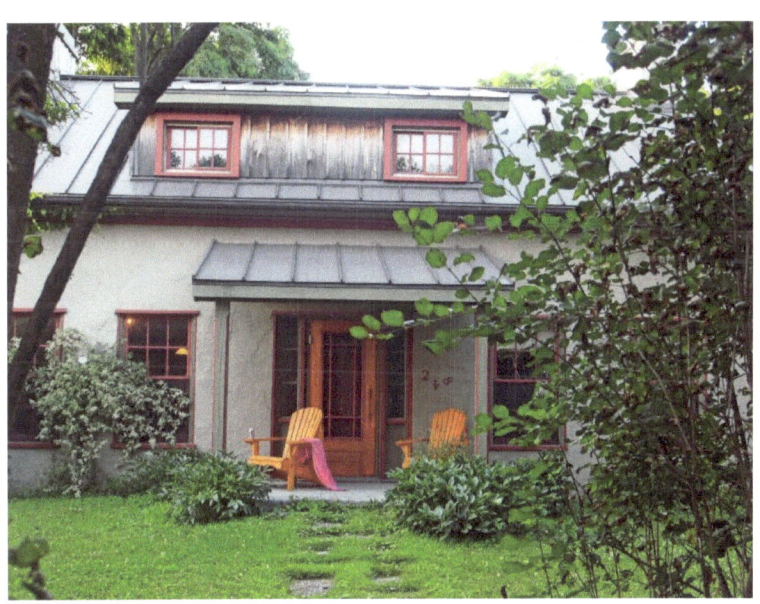

248 James Street – shed dormer, sidelights,
6-over-6 window panes

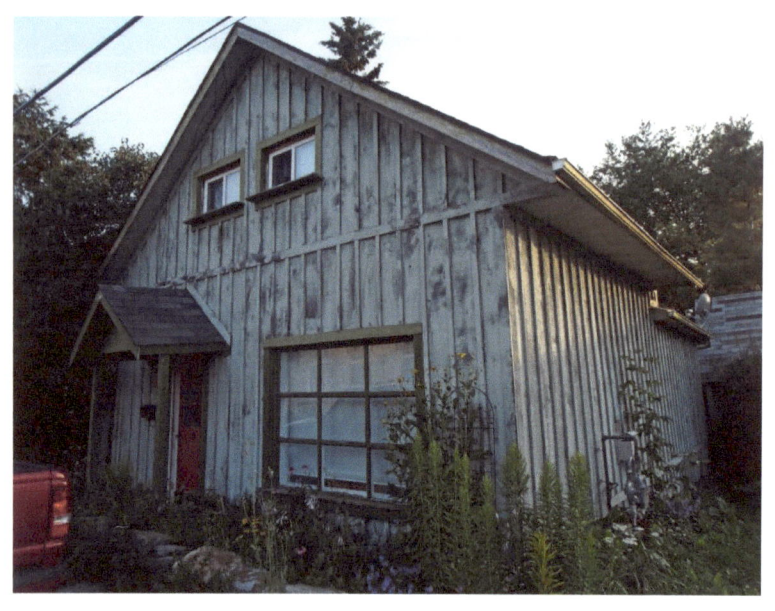

3 Drummond Street – 1½ storey board and batten

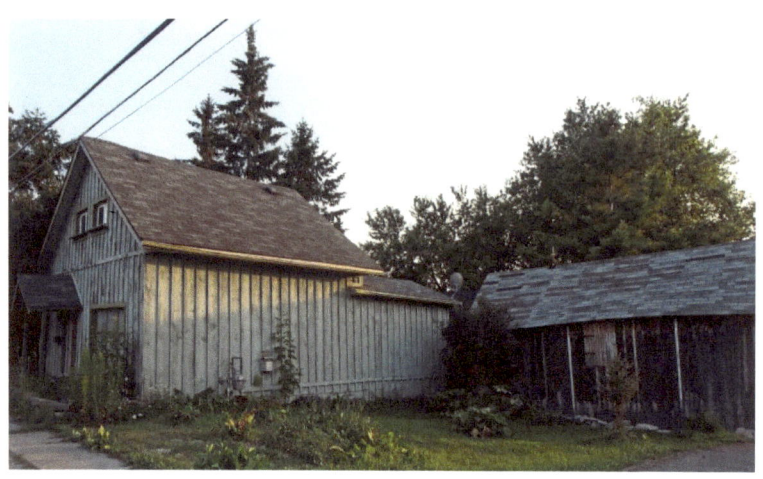

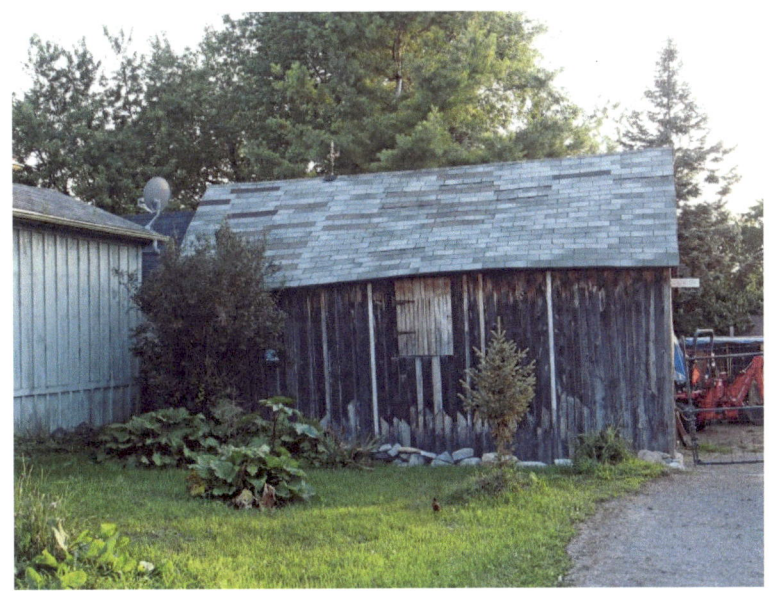

3 Drummond Street – shed

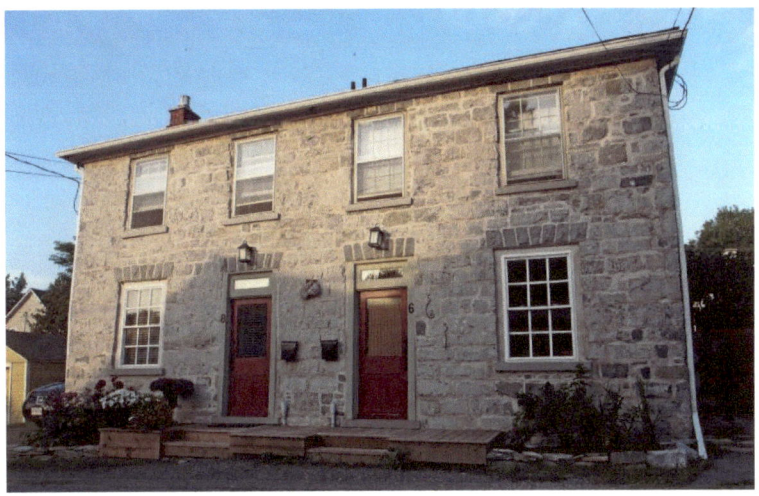

6-8 Drummond Street – two-storey limestone, 6-over-6
window panes, transom windows above doors

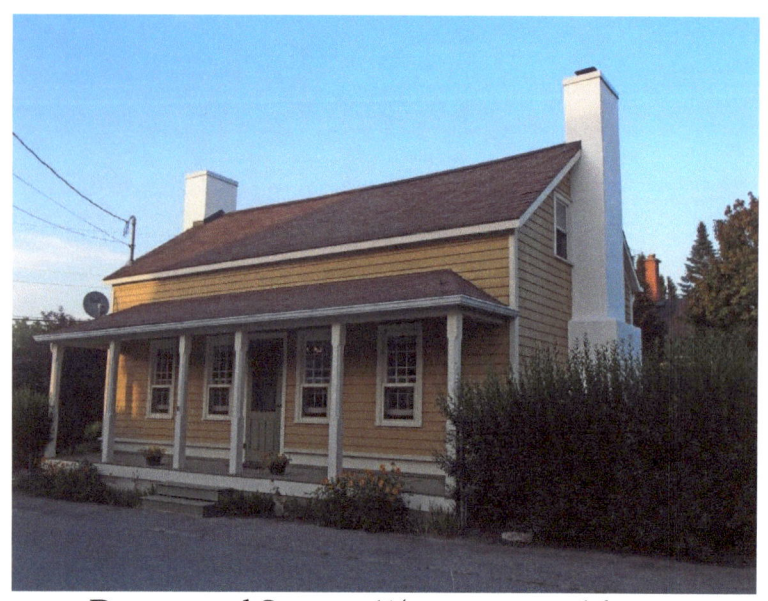

Drummond Street – 1½ storey wood frame

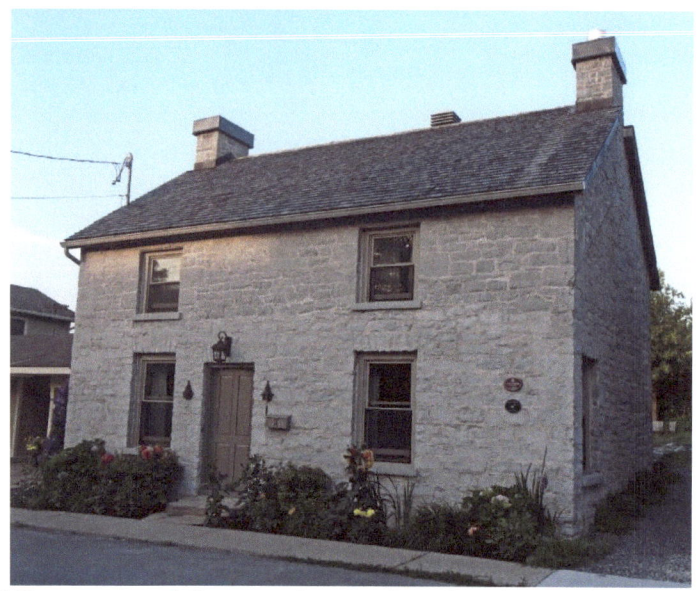

14 Drummond Street – James Pentland, Cordwainer (a shoemaker who makes new shoes from new leather) – 1830 – 1½ storey Gothic Revival - limestone

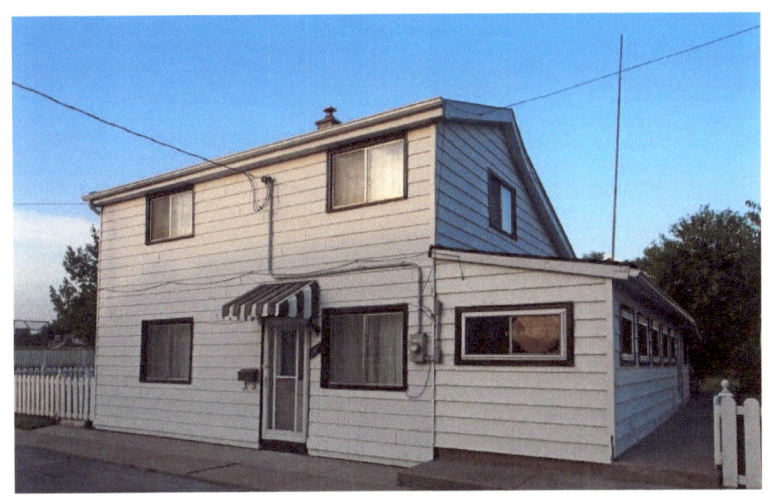

18 Drummond Street

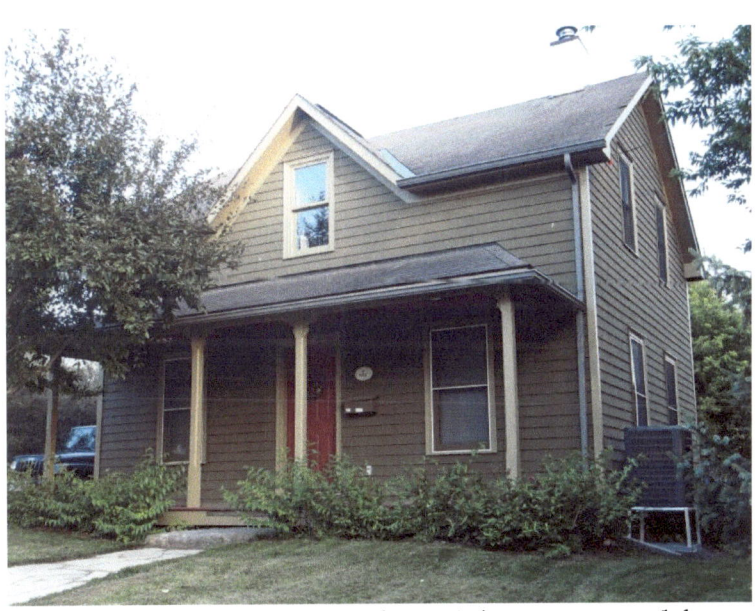

402 Wellington Street – Gothic – 1½ storey wood frame

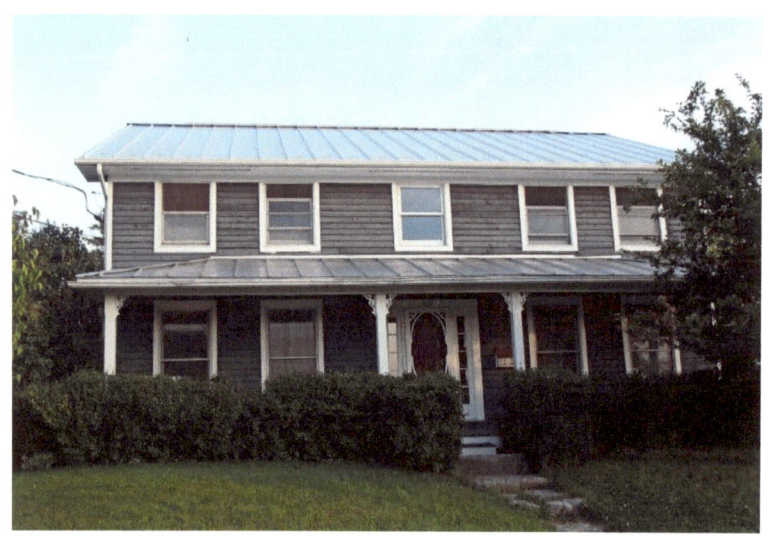

408 Wellington Street – two storeys, sidelights

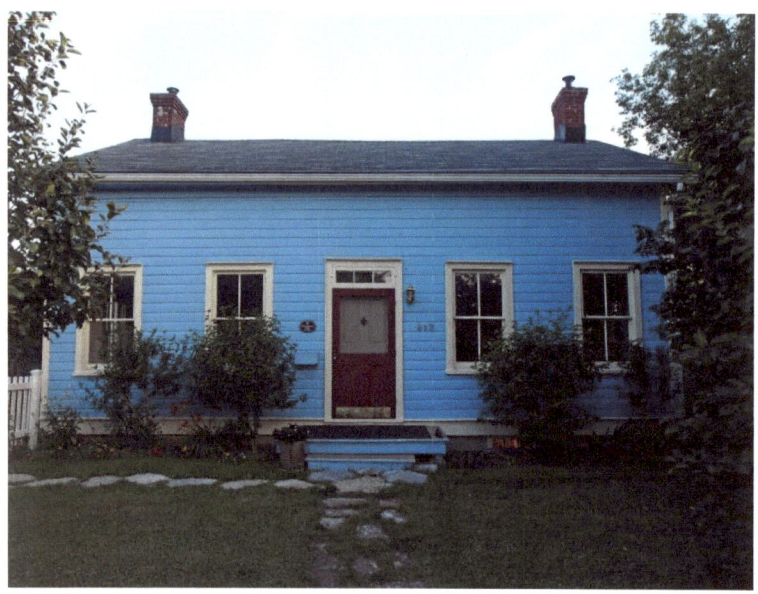

412 Wellington Street – William Allan House – 1860
– one storey wood frame, transom window

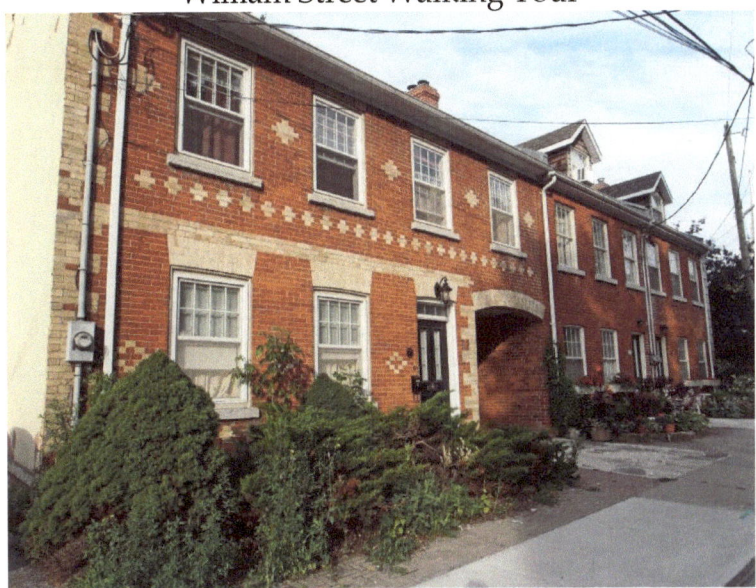

112 William Street – 1857 – light brick set against red brick in Greek cross and lozenge patterns to separate windows and storeys; arched carriageway led to stables

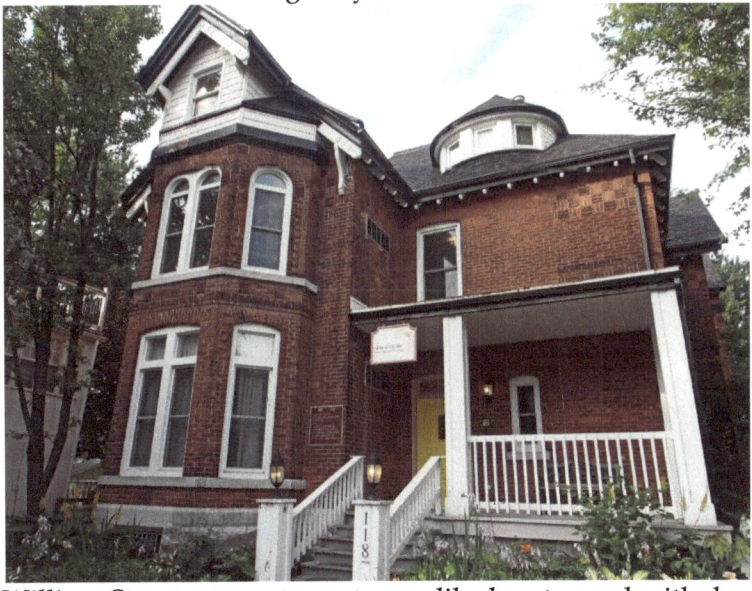

118 William Street – two-storey tower-like bay topped with dormer, unusual shaped dormer to right

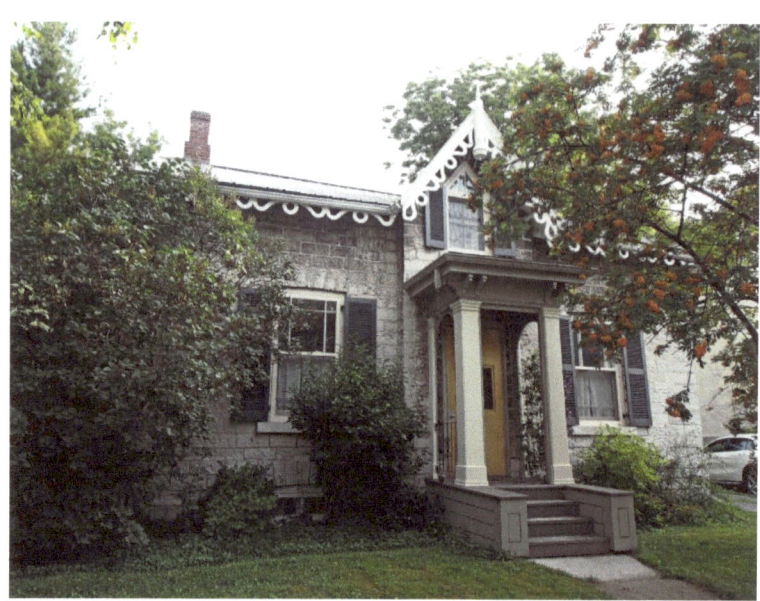

129 William Street – 1870 – limestone Regency Cottage – decorative bargeboards with finial on gable, columned entranceway

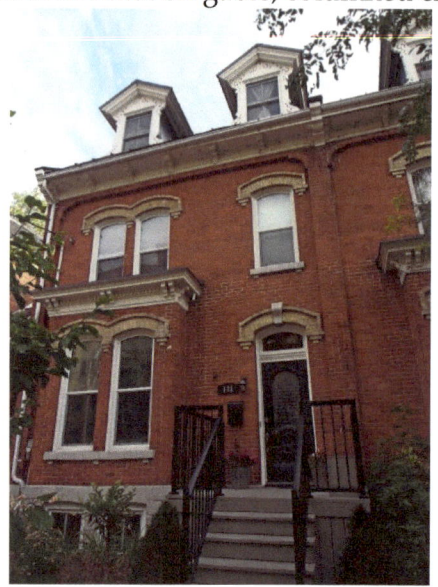

141 William Street – rectangular bay window with arched voussoirs, cornice brackets and dentil moulding; dormers in roof; voussoirs with keystone and transom window above door

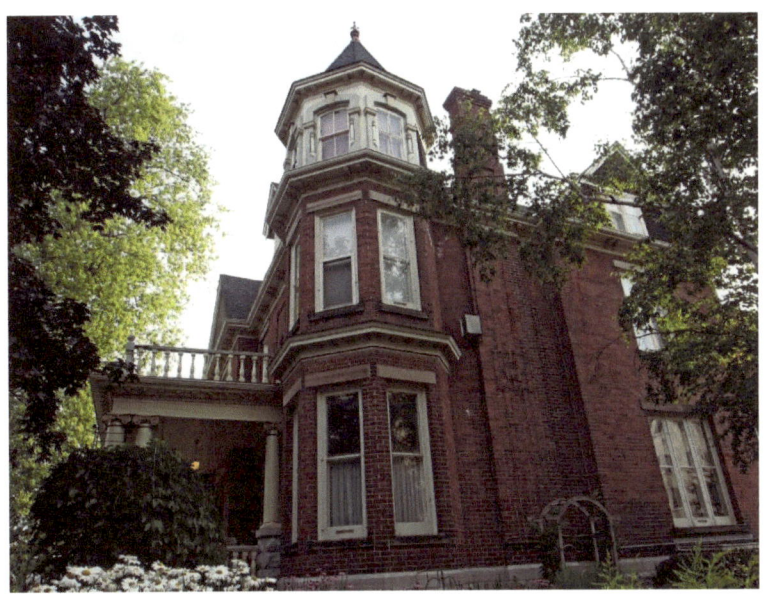

73 Sydenham at corner of William Street – The Secret Garden Bed and Breakfast – two-storey brick – 1888 – Victorian - terra cotta (hard, kiln-fired clay) decoration at second floor level; bargeboards on west dormer; three-storey tower; Ionic columns supporting verandah

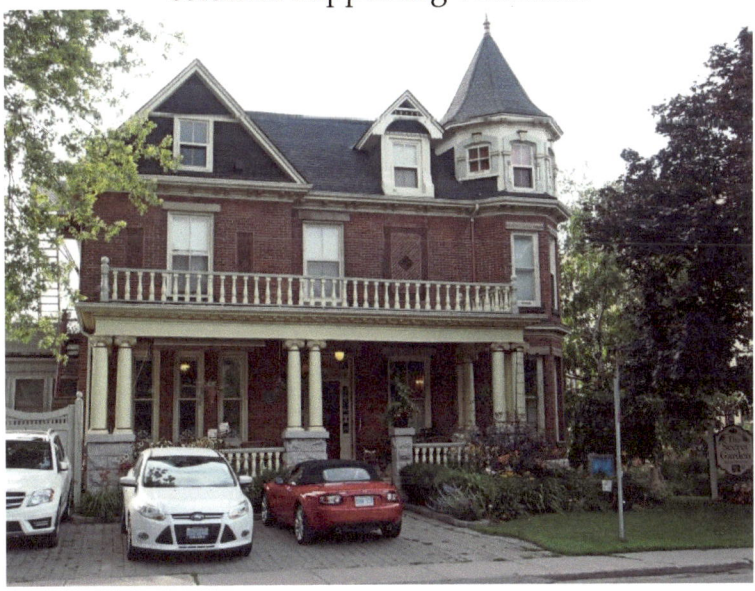

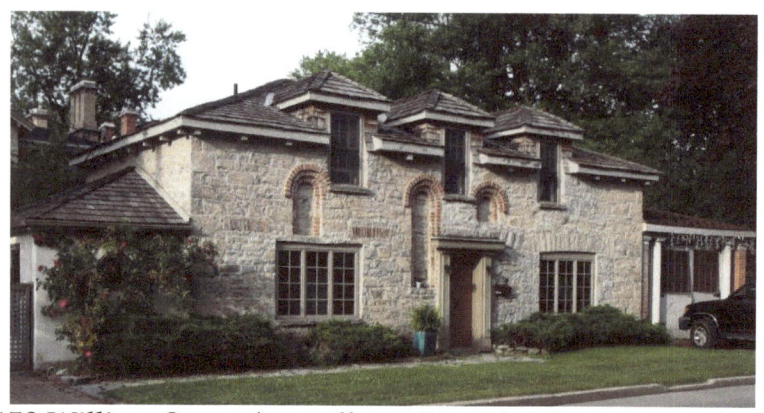

150 William Street (as well as 186 and 170) – were stables converted to private homes – built from cobblestone, hip roof, 1½ storeys - #150 was the stable for 46 Sydenham Street around the corner

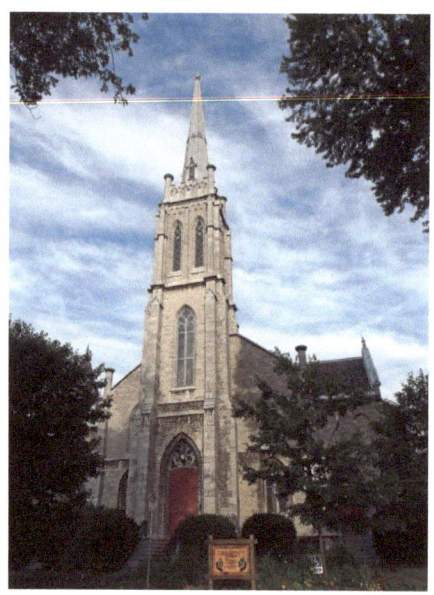

Sydenham Street United Church – built for Wesleyan Methodists in 1851 – Gothic Revival style – stone – central tower is buttressed and rises to a spire topped by a finial, arched windows and doors have intricate details

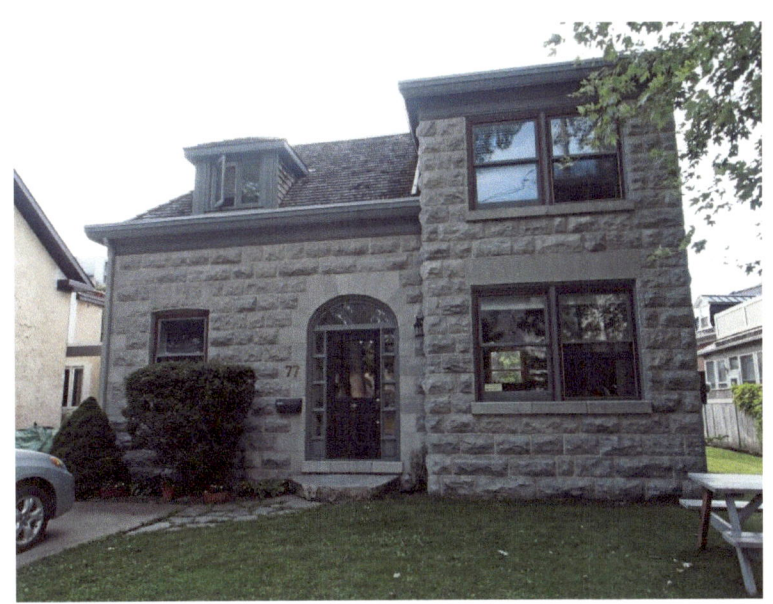

77 Sydenham Street - dormer

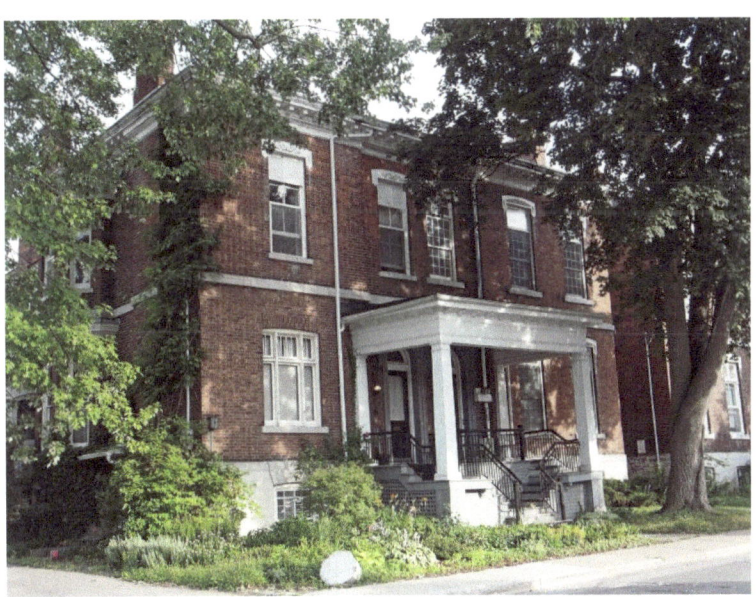

86-88 Sydenham Street – 1879 – two-storey red brick

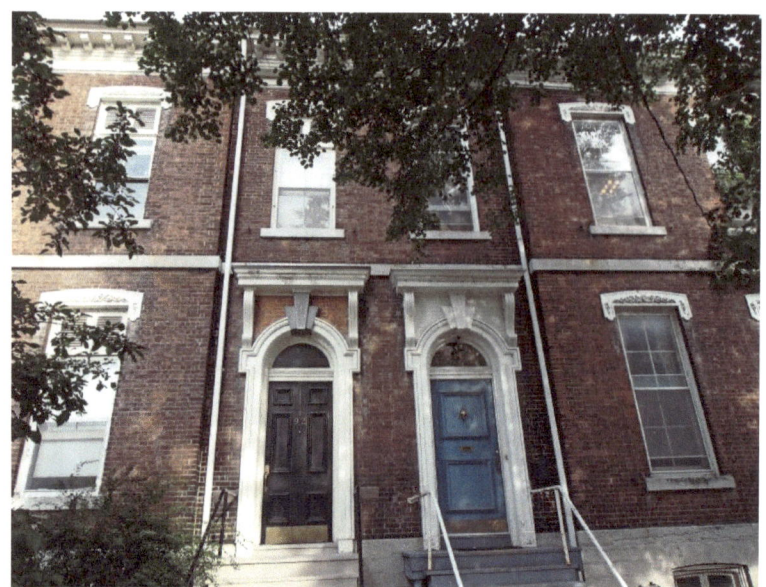

92-94 Sydenham Street – two storey red brick, hoods above doors, transom windows

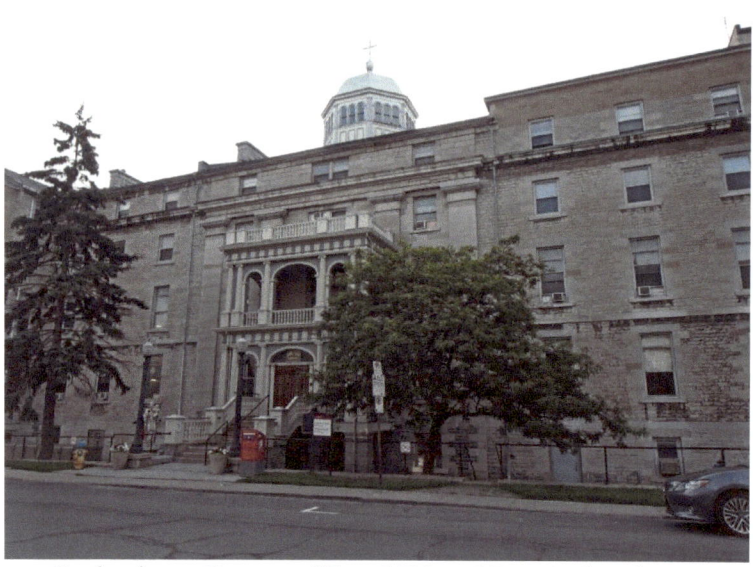

Sydenham Street – Hotel Dieu Hospital – dome

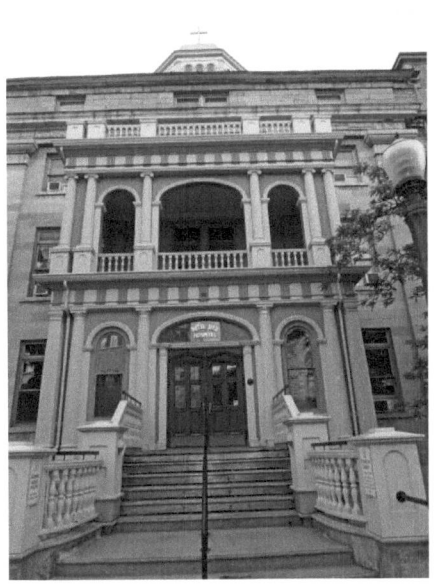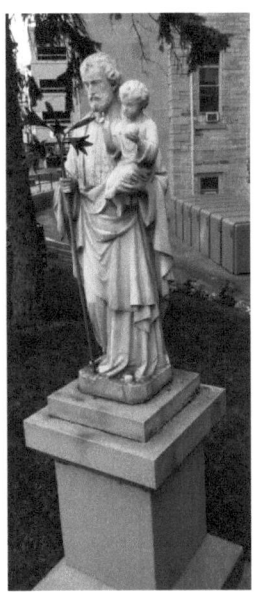

Regiopolis College, incorporated March 4, 1837, opened in the
central portion of this building. In 1866, the college was given
full degree-granting powers. Financial difficulties forced its
closing in 1869. In 1892 the building was acquired by the
Religious Hospitallers of St. Joseph who opened here the
Hotel Dieu Hospital. The school reopened on King Street in
1896, and in 1915 moved to the northern part of the city. In
1931 the diocesan clergy transferred the college to the Jesuit
Order.

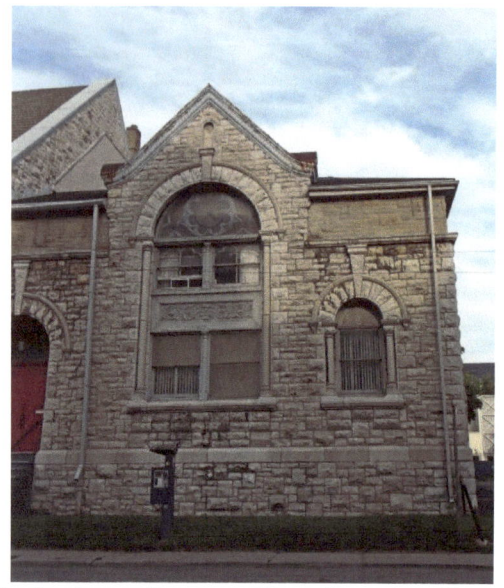
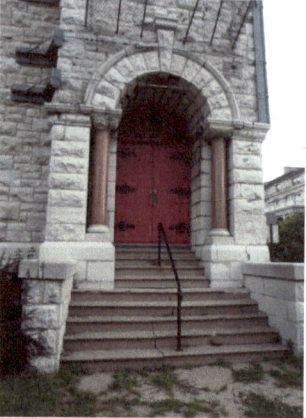

Sydenham Street – First Baptist Church – 1913 – Romanesque style – voussoirs with keystones, Ionic pillars surrounding entrance

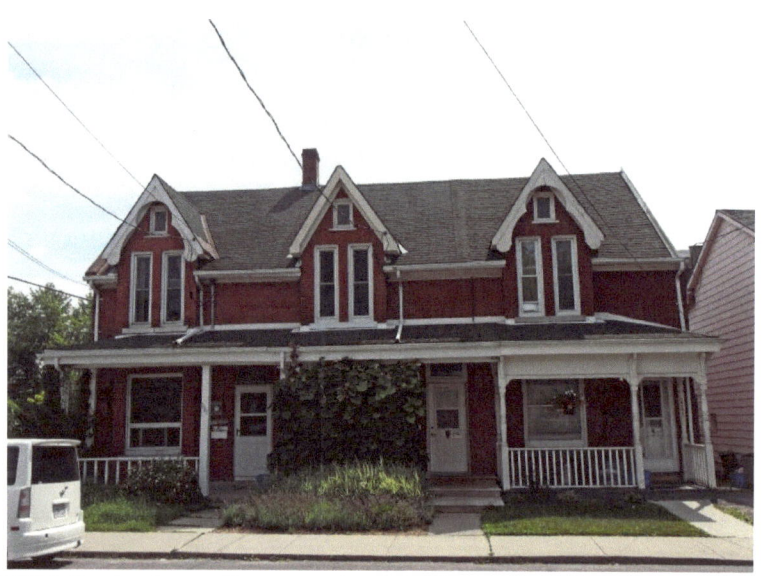

217-221 Sydenham Street – Gothic, bargeboard trim on gables

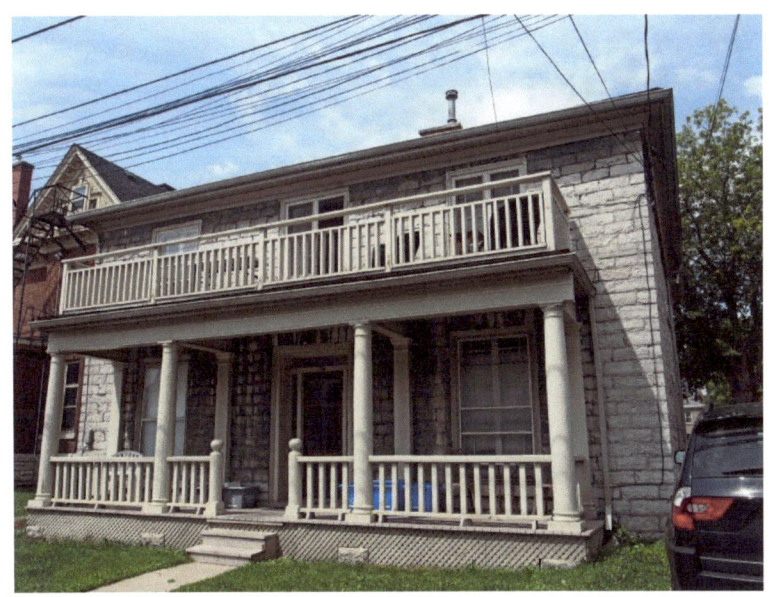

210 Sydenham Street – two storeys, second floor balcony

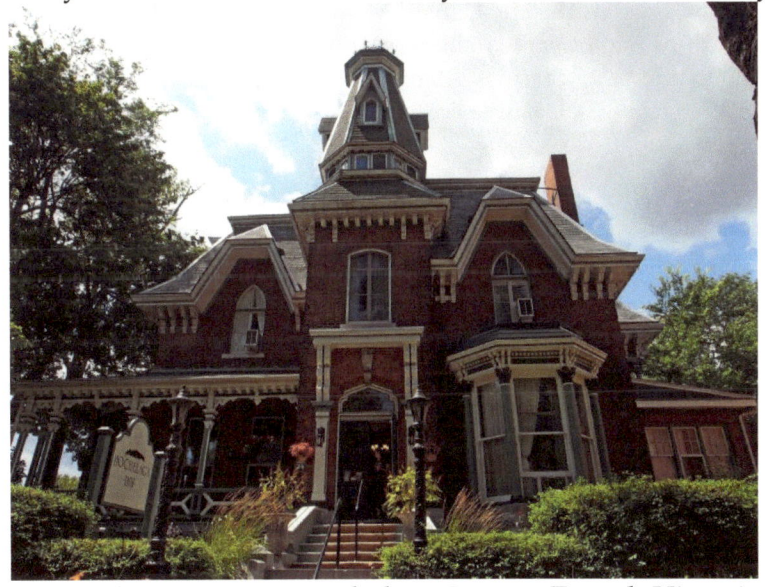

24 Sydenham Street – Hochelaga Inn – a French Victorian mansion built in 1879 by John McIntyre and his wife Harriet, who was a relative of Sir John A. Macdonald – transformed into an inn in 1985 – three-storey tower, cornice brackets, bay window

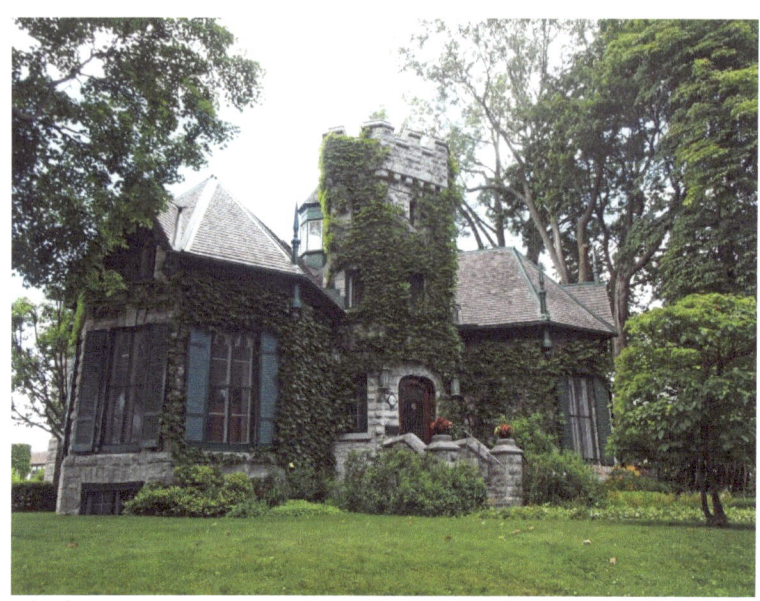

14 Sydenham Street – McIntosh Castle – built 1852 – Gothic Revival style - commissioned in 1850 by Donald McIntosh, who owned a couple of steamships that traversed Lake Ontario between Kingston, Toronto, Hamilton and St. Catharines. McIntosh promised his wife a castle if she agreed to leave their native Scotland to find their fortune in Canada.

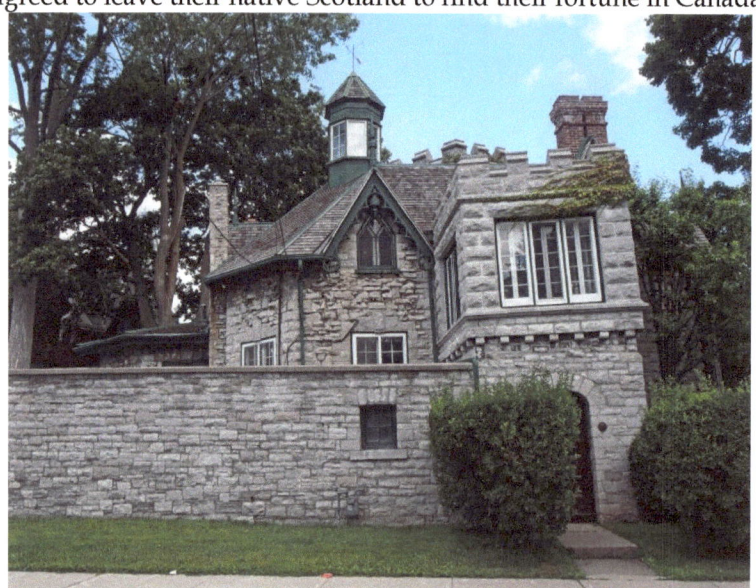

Cupola

Architectural Terms

Bay Window: A window that projects out from a wall, in a semicircular, rectangular, or polygonal design. Used frequently in Gothic and Victorian designs. Example: 148 Barrie Street, Page 16	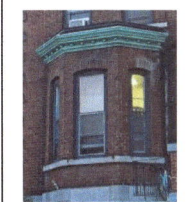
Brackets: a decorative or weight-bearing structural element which forms a right angle with one side against a wall and the other under a projecting surface such as an eave or roof. Example: 24 Sydenham Street, Page 61	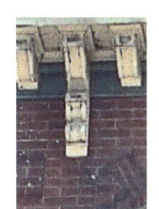
Buttress: a masonry structure built against or projecting from a wall which serves to support or reinforce the wall. In Canadian architecture, they are sometimes used for decoration. Example: 965 Sydenham Road, Cataraqui, Page 12	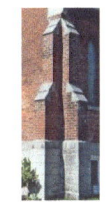

Capital: The uppermost finish or decoration on a column. An Ionic column has a small base, a thin elegant shaft, and a capital composed of carved whirls or twists that take the form of a scroll. Example: 18 Barrie Street. A Doric column has a plain column with a simple capital. Example: 68-70 Barrie Street. A Corinthian column has a rounded capital decorated with acanthus leaves on tall slender columns. Example: 212 Barrie Street	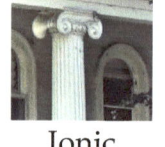 Ionic 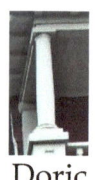 Doric 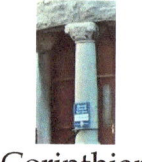 Corinthian
Cobblestone architecture: Refers to the use of cobblestones embedded in mortar as a method for erecting walls on houses and commercial buildings. Example: 234 James Street, Barriefield Village, Page 31	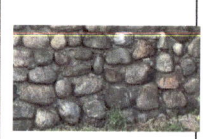
Cornice Return: decorative element on the end of a gable. Example: Sharman's Lane, Barriefield, Page 39	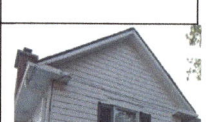
Cupola: A domed or curved roof rising from a building as a decorative element. Example: 911 Purdy Mills Road, Cataraqui, Page 14	
Dentil Moulding: an even series of rectangles used as ornamental decoration in cornices. Example: 141 William Street, Page 54	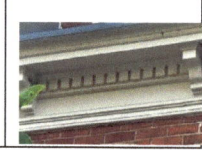

Dormer: (French for "sleep") a gable end window that pierces through the plane of a sloping roof surface to create usable space in the top floor or attic of a building by adding headroom. Example: 62 Barrie Street, Page 17	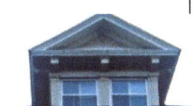
Entrance: The entrance encompasses the doorway and the inner vestibule or, in residential architecture, the covered porch. Example: Sydenham Street, Page 60	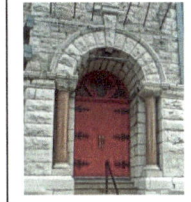
Frontispiece: a portion of the façade of a building, usually a centred doorway that is slightly raised from the rest of the building, usually has extensive ornamentation. Frontispieces are usually Classical in design with white columned porches. Example: 331-333 Barrie Street, Page 25	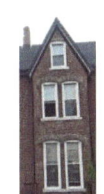
Gable: the triangular portion of a wall between the edges of a sloping roof. Example: 983 Sydenham Road, Cataraqui, Page 11	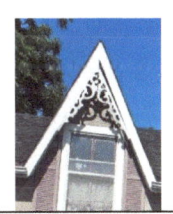
Hipped Roof: a roof where all sides slope downwards to the walls with no gables. Example: 247 Main Street, Page 27	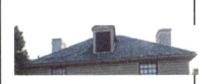
Iron Cresting: A decorative ornament along the top of a roof. Iron cresting was popular in the Baroque era and also in Italianate, Victorian, Second Empire and Queen Anne styles of architecture. Example: 72-74 Barrie Street, Page 18	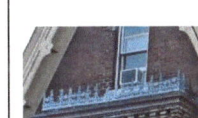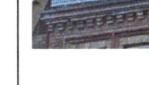

Keystones and Voussoirs: a voussoir is a wedge-shaped element used in building an arch. A keystone is the central stone that locks all the stones into position, allowing the arch to bear weight. A keystone is often enlarged and embellished. Example: Sydenham Street, Pg. 60	
Lancet Window: a tall, narrow window with a pointed arch at its top. Example: 974 Sydenham Road, Cataraqui, Page 10	
Mansard Roof: This style was popularized by Francois Mansart (1598-1666), an accomplished architect of the French Baroque period and especially fashionable during the Second French Empire (1852-1870). This roof is almost flat on the top section, with two slopes on each of its sides with the lower slope at a steeper angle than the upper and having dormer windows. Example: 148 Barrie Street, Page 16	
Palladian Window: a large window that is divided into three sections with the centre section larger than the two side sections and usually arched. Example: 28 Barrie Street, Page 16	
Pediment: a triangular section above the horizontal structure (entablature), typically supported by columns. The inside of the triangle is called the tympanum. Example: 62 Barrie Street, Page 17	

The **quatrefoil** is a type of decorative framework consisting of a symmetrical shape which forms the outline of four partially overlapping circles of the same diameter. The word quatrefoil comes from Latin and means "four leaves". Example: 212 Barrie Street, Page 21	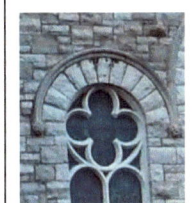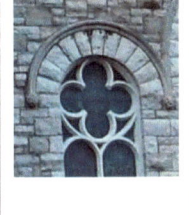
Quoin: masonry blocks at the corner of a wall, often a decorative feature, usually larger or of a different colour than the rest of the wall. Example: 72-74 Barrie Street, Page 18	
Rose Window: a circular window with ornamental tracery radiating from the centre. Example: 212 Barrie Street, Page 21	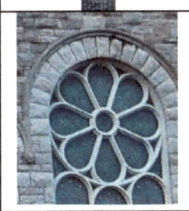
Sidelight: a window, usually with a vertical emphasis, that flanks a door, and is often used to emphasize the importance of a primary entrance. **Transom Window:** the light above the doorway, also called a fanlight. Example: 80 Barrie Street, Page 19	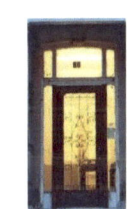
Verge board and Finial: also called bargeboards – hang from the projecting end of a roof and are often elaborately carved and ornamented. **Finial:** ornament added to the top of a gable, pinnacle, canopy or spire – a Gothic element. Example: 232 James Street, Page 33	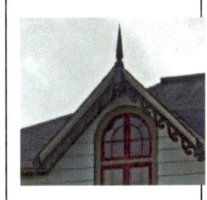
Window Hood: the piece found above window openings, usually of an ornate design, and covers the top third of the opening. Hoods are commonly placed above arched or curved openings on both windows and doors. Example: 307 Barrie Street, Page 23	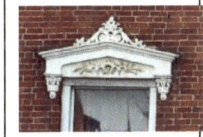

Classical Revival (1820 - 1860) – This style was an analytical, scientific, and dogmatic revival based on intensive studies of Greek and Roman buildings, concerned with the application of Greek plans and proportions to civic buildings. Schools, libraries, government offices, and most other civic buildings were built in the Classical Revival style. The white columned porches of the Classical Revival domestic buildings are identified with the mansions of wealthy land owners in Canada. Example: 18 Barrie Street, Page 14	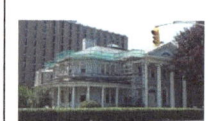
Edwardian, 1900-1930 – This style bridges the ornate and elaborate styles of the Victorian era and the simplified styles of the 20th century. Balanced facades, simple roof lines, dormer windows, large front porches, and smooth brick surfaces are its characteristics. Example: 26 Barrie Street, Page 15	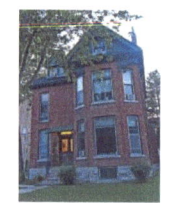
Gothic Revival, 1830-1890 – These decorative buildings have sharply-pitched gables with highly detailed verge boards, pointed-arch window openings, and dichromatic brickwork. It is a common style in Ontario. Example: 72-74 Barrie Street, Page 18	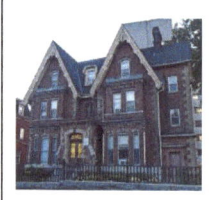

A **log cabin**, built from logs, was usually one- or 1½-storeys constructed with round rather than hewn, or hand-worked, logs, and erected quickly for frontier shelter. Log cabins were built from logs laid horizontally and interlocked on the ends with notches. The cabin was situated to provide sunlight and drainage so the pioneers could cope better with the rigors of frontier life. The pioneers chose old-growth trees that were straight and had few knots and did not need to be hewn to fit well together. The length of one log was the length of one wall.
Example: Green Bay Road, Page 34

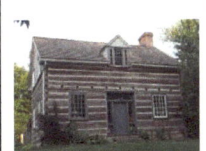

Italianate, 1850-1900 – A two story rectangular building with a mild hip roof, a projecting frontispiece, and generous eaves with ornate cornice brackets was the basis of the style; often there are large sash windows, quoins, ornate detailing on the windows, belvederes and wraparound verandahs. Italianate commercial buildings often have cast iron cresting and elegant window surrounds.
Example: 80 Barrie Street, Page 19

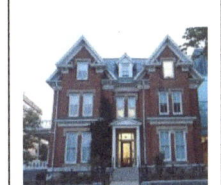

Queen Anne, 1885-1900 – This style is distinguished by an irregular outline featuring a combination of an offset tower, broad gables, projecting two-storey bays, verandahs, multi-sloped roofs, and tall, decorative chimneys. A mixture of brick and wood is common. Windows often have one large single-paned bottom sash and small panes in the upper sash. Example: 78 Barrie Street, Page 19

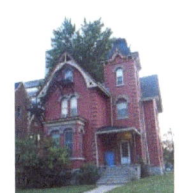

Regency Cottage, 1830-1860 – This style originated in England in 1815 and spread to Ontario later in the 19th century as British officers retired to Canada. It is a modest one-storey house with a low-pitched hip roof and has a symmetrical front façade. Example: 129 William Street, Page 54	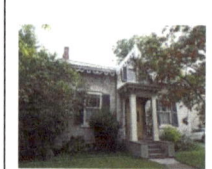
Romanesque Revival, 1880-1910 – This style hearkens back to medieval architecture of the 11th and 12th centuries with a heavy appearance, blocky towers and rounded arches. Example: 212 Barrie Street, Page 21	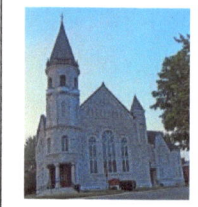
Second Empire, 1860-1880 – The mansard roof is the most noteworthy feature of this style and is evidence of the French origins. Projecting central towers and one or two-storey bays can also be present. Example: 148 Barrie Street, Page 16	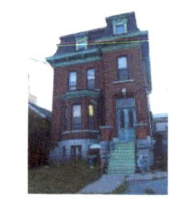
Victorian - In Ontario, a Victorian style building can be seen as any building built between 1840 and 1900 that doesn't fit into any of the other categories. It encompasses a large group of buildings constructed in brick, stone, and timber, using an eclectic mixture of Classical and Gothic motifs. Example: 24 Sydenham Street, Page 61	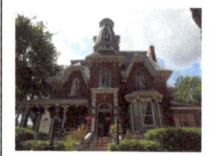

www.ingramcontent.com/pod-product-compliance
Lightning Source LLC
Chambersburg PA
CBHW040837180526
45159CB00001B/223